Collins

LITTLE BOOKS

RUM

HarperCollins Publishers
Westerhill Road
Bishopbriggs
Glasgow
G64 2QT

First Edition 2018

10 9 8 7 6 5 4 3 2 1

© HarperCollins Publishers 2018

ISBN 978-0-00-827122-0

Collins® is a registered trademark
of HarperCollins Publishers Limited

www.collins.co.uk

A catalogue record for this book is
available from the British Library

Author: Dominic Roskrow

Typeset by
Davidson Publishing Solutions

Printed and bound in China by
RR Donnelley APS Co Ltd

MIX
Paper from
responsible sources
FSC™ C007454

This book is produced from independently certified FSC™ paper
to ensure responsible forest management.

For more information visit: www.harpercollins.co.uk/green

Contents

About the Author

Dominic Roskrow is an award-winning drinks writer and magazine editor. He specialises in whisky and has written 12 books on the subject. He has edited *The Spirits Business*, *Club Mirror*, *Pub Business*, and *Whisky Magazine*, writes a spirits column for *Drinks International*, and has contributed to dozens of newspapers and magazines across the world. He was Fortnum & Mason Drinks Writer of the Year in 2015. His most recent book, *Whisky: Japan*, was chosen as Britain's best spirits book in the Gourmand Food and Drink Awards and is shortlisted for the title of Gourmand World's Best Spirit Book.

Dominic is one of only a few people to be chosen as a Keeper of the Quaich for his work on Scotch whisky, and to be appointed a Kentucky Colonel for his promotion of bourbon. Dominic is an avid Leicester City and All Blacks fan, and loves loud heavy rock music.

Rum set to step into the spotlight

Given the continued success of the cocktail culture, a seemingly limitless demand for craft alcoholic drinks, and the demand from consumers for drinks with heritage and provenance, it's tempting to say that rum is set to become fashionable again.

But it would be wrong to do so, mainly because while rum may not have spent a great deal of time in the spotlight, it has never left the stage either. Those old enough to remember the 1970s will recall that Bacardi and Coke and Rum and Black were highly popular, even back then. And by the time the mullet, shoulder pads and white trouser brigade were strutting their stuff at Club Tropicana with Wham in the 1980s, rum was the cocktail spirit of choice.

True, vodka was the dominant spirit when bartenders got serious and decided they were now mixologists. And when drinking spirits was reinvented as an art form, it was Scottish single malt and Japanese whisky that benefited.

But rum never really went away. It is the chameleon of the drinks world, changing its skin to survive in different drinking climates. At the populist end of the drinks spectrum it is represented by cheap and cheerful cartoon pirate brands. When we started taking exotic holidays it was all about rum on luxury yachts, next to crystal-blue water and reclining on white sandy beaches. When the Spice Girls were doing their thing, what we really really wanted was spiced rums.

When we started to premiumise our drinks, rum was there, the more traditional expressions riffing on a Royal Navy history that included a rum ration given to every sailor at midday for an amazing 230 years, until the ration was scrapped in 1970. The day it was stopped, 31 July, is marked by Black Tot Day. Rum is the only positive in the description of life in the Royal Navy as 'rum, sodomy and the lash', and a century before that the pirate link was established, as monarch-endorsed buccaneers set out to loot the ships of rival nations as they sought to trade in the Americas and across the Caribbean. There is an unsavoury side to the period, too, because much of the attraction of the Caribbean was, indeed, rum (and the sugar it was produced from), and the currency to purchase it was African slaves.

Rum is the drinks industry's ultimate mistress, seductively whispering in the ear of bartenders everywhere 'I'll be whatever you want me to be.' It is the ultimate multicultural spirit, available in white, brown, golden and dark formats. It is normally sweet with toffee and vanilla notes, but it can be oaky, fruity and spicy. It can be a cheap mixing spirit, or an expensive sipping one. There are standard and premium versions of it. It can be a loveable puppy of a spirit, all youthful exuberance and frolicsome fun, but it can be as venerable an old man as any Scottish single malt. You want the spirits equivalent of a Take That concert? Then a standard rum with coke or in a cocktail will do the trick. But if, metaphorically, a virtuoso performance at the Albert Hall is more your thing, then search out one of the rare and aged rums that are best enjoyed slowly and with respect.

Rum is a remarkably resilient spirit, and seems to have found endless ways of reinventing itself. Today its future lies in three distinct areas.

Firstly, like all spirits with a good back story, the sector is benefitting from the current demand for brands that have heritage and history. Consumers are drinking less but better, and are not necessarily after cheap so much as value for money. And any drink that can show that it comes from a specific location, has been produced successfully for generations, or has a bond with a specific place or family, will attract interest. Increasingly, enjoyment of spirits has strayed way beyond just drinking them, and has grown into a hobby. Discerning drinkers want to know how each drink is made, what its unique selling points are, and where the distillery is – a remote location on a West Indian island or in the forests of Venezuela fits the bill perfectly.

Secondly, related to that is the desire of drinkers to discover new styles, and to appreciate the nuances between different rums. Rum is made across the world but there is a concentration of production in the Caribbean and Central America. Undoubtedly there are differences in rums from different West Indian islands and, in particular, the rums from Cuba.

The changing relationship Cuba has with the West – on hold again in the United States with the election of a hostile administration – raises the potential for Cuba to export some of its more esoteric and exciting creations.

There is also a growing interest in specialist rums from the French-controlled regions of the Caribbean, particularly Martinique. Here they make a style of rum called rhum agricole, which is rum distilled from freshly-squeezed sugarcane juice rather than molasses, and it is a very different style of rum to the caramel-coated expressions we tend to associate with commercial rums.

And finally, the craft distilling boom provides a platform for niche rums. The trendiest bars will search for spirits that set them apart from their competitors – and at the most serious end of the bar scene, drinks makers are either making their own rums or working with micro-distillers to do so.

Many of these rums have been created to work in specific house cocktails and, like home-produced bitters, are designed to ensure that the bar's best cocktails can't be copied elsewhere. That said, the owners of bars such as Bramble Bar in Edinburgh have now started making their own spirits, including rum, and are selling them through what they describe as 'one of the world's smallest drinks retailers'.

So rum is in rude good health, and with many predicting a surge in interest in premium rums, particularly premium white rums, the category can grow even stronger.

What is rum and how is it made?

Rum is a a spirit distilled from sugarcane by-products such as fermented molasses, which are thick and syrupy, or from freshly-squeezed sugarcane juices. Rum is not the easiest spirit to make because of the viscosity of the raw materials. First, the molasses or juices must be fermented, and this is done by adding yeast to feed on the sugars, creating alcohol and carbon dioxide. The fermented liquid is then distilled, producing a clear liquid. This may be marketed as rum and is used mainly for mixing and for cocktails. But rum may be aged in oak barrels to create a premium rum, which is best consumed straight or over ice. Rum can be, and is, made in any country that produces sugarcane, but it is its commonly associated with the Caribbean.

Rums made from sugarcane juices are significantly different to common rums and are particularly associated with the French regions of the Caribbean (rhum agricoles) and with Brazil (cachaca).

Alcohol strength

The rules governing rum are not as stringent as the rules governing Scotch whisky, and the strength of rums vary from 37.5% ABV to 80.0% plus. But different countries define rum differently. For instance, in the United States rum must be a minimum of 80% proof – 40.0% ABV.

Some countries also demand that rum is matured in oak barrels for a minimum length of time.

Styles of rum

White rum

White rum is the entry point for many people new to the rum category. In many cases it is young rum that mixes easily and is the base for mainstream rum cocktails. It is a category dominated by Bacardi, one of the world's most successful spirit brands.

But if ever there was a drinks category that defied the idea that the darker a spirit, the more flavoursome and older it is, this is it. There are several examples of superior rums that are clear, and drinks experts predict that premium white rum is set to become a trendsetter in coming years. There are white rums that have been matured for several years and their colour, but not their superior taste, has been stripped out.

Golden rum

Of all spirits categories rum is quite possibly the most lawless, which is a status it is happy to keep, given its rebellious and wild image. So there is no formal definition of what a golden rum is, but it is regarded as a halfway house between white rums and dark rums, and will have benefitted from some ageing. It is generally considered to be more complex than many white rums.

Dark rum

Dark rum at its best refers to rum that has been aged for a considerable time, possibly in heavily charred oak barrels. Dark rum is designed to be consumed in the same way as a single malt whisky. Dark rums may be aged for many years. But the category also refers to the very sweet Demerara style of rum, most commonly associated with Guyana. This style formed the base for the rums served on Royal Navy ships and served in British pubs.

Spiced rum

Normally a spiced rum gets its flavours from spices being added after distillation. There are two reasons for this: firstly, distillation will remove much of the flavour of the spices; and secondly, because the spicy flavours left in the still will affect the taste of the next distillation. Spices used include cloves, nutmeg, cinnamon, star anise, peppercorns, citrus peel zest, and ginger.

Rhum agricole

Rhum agricole is rum made in the French Caribbean islands, produced from fermented sugarcane juice and with a distinctive, earthy and more grassy flavour than standard rum.

Cachaca

The national drink of Brazil is a form of rum distilled from fermented sugarcane juice.

RUM

Ableforth's Rumbullion! 15 Years Old

PRODUCER: Atom Supplies

AREA OF ORIGIN: Tonbridge Wells, England

VARIETY: Spiced rum

ABV: 46.2%

WEBSITE: www.ableforths.com

Ableforth's Rumbullion 15 Years Old is one of the most thrilling and outstanding rums on the market, not because it is the very best, or the coolest, or the most popular, or the most fun, but because it contains elements of all those attributes, making it a truly great all-rounder. Rumbullion!'s creators have a healthy, irreverent approach to the world of spirits, and there's something very playful about this delicious-tasting rum. It is loaded with Christmas spices, tastes wonderful in a trifle, and as a stand-alone drink, having won the title of the world's best spiced rum in the past. Packaging-wise, it's as cool as rum gets. Like the original, the 15-year-old is a rich blend of vanilla, orange peel and fine spices, but the extra years give it an oaky, rich and more complex flavour. Excellent.

Ableforth's Rumbullion! Navy-Strength

PRODUCER: Atom Supplies

AREA OF ORIGIN: Tonbridge Wells, England

VARIETY: Spiced rum

ABV: 57.0%

WEBSITE: www.ableforths.com

There are plenty of drinks authorities who think that rum is set for a place in the drinks spotlight. It has always been a favourite with bartenders because it mixes so well, but with many spirits drinkers turned off by the high price of single malt, there is a feeling that sipping and aged rums are ideally placed to take advantage of the desire for well made spirits with their own personality and with heritage and provenance. If there's been a problem with the category it's that the rules governing what is and isn't rum are lax, and standards vary considerably across the sector. Rumbullion! Navy-Strength has no such worries. This version isn't just greater in strength, it's bigger in flavour, too. Cardamom and cloves join the orange and vanilla hit of its sister expressions.

Admiral Vernon's Old J Tiki Fire

PRODUCER: LWC

AREA OF ORIGIN: London, England

VARIETY: Golden spiced rum

ABV: 75.5%

WEBSITE: www.oldjspicedrum.co.uk

This super strength rum is ironically named, because Admiral Edward Vernon weakened the strength of the daily rum ration from its Navy Strength of 57.0% ABV. Navy Strength is the strength of rum needed for gunpowder doused in it to catch fire when lit. Any weaker ABV meant that the rum or gin had been diluted. Not surprisingly, the men weren't happy with the change, and when they complained Vernon told them to add lime and sugar to make the weaker grog more palatable. That's what's happening here. Lime, vanilla and sugar mark out this rum, as well as a strong spicy note. Old J Tiki Fire is a high-strength version of Old J Spiced Rum, and the added strength means that Old J Tiki Fire makes its presence felt in a whole host of rum-based cocktails. Obviously not to be consumed neat.

Alnwick White Knight

PRODUCER: Alnwick Rum Company

AREA OF ORIGIN: Alnwick, England

VARIETY: White rum

ABV: 37.5%

WEBSITE: www.lindisfarne-mead.co.uk/AlnwickRum

Alnwick – pronounced Ann-ick – is a small town in Northumberland, in the far North East of England. Offshore is Lindisfarne, an island that is home to monks, countless seabirds, and alcohol production, especially mead. The Alnwick Rum Company fits right in here, and has successfully made dark rums that are sold in the region in selected drinks outlets, and online. White Knight is the company's white rum and, as there is a view that quality and niche white rums are becoming increasingly fashionable, White Knight ticks all the right boxes. White Knight is a white Guyanese rum brought down to bottling strength with spring water from the Northumberland hills. It is fruity, easy drinking and has soft toffee notes.

Angostura 1787

PRODUCER: Angostura Holdings Limited

AREA OF ORIGIN: Trinidad and Tobago

VARIETY: Premium dark rum

ABV: 40.0%

WEBSITE: www.angosturarum.com

Different suppliers and producers take vastly different approaches to the marketing of rum, from pirates to parties, and from cheap and cheerful to classy connoisseur. Angostura is in the serious category. It points out that all of its rum comes from just one distillery in Trinidad, in the same way that a single malt whisky derives from one place, it says – only its rum is better. That's obviously a big claim but taste this and you can see the company has an argument. This was released in the second half of 2016 and is 15 years old. You can taste the oak in the rum, and there are some impressive tannin and spice notes. There are some exotic and dried berry fruits on the palate, too, as well as toffee. A balanced, rounded and excellent quality rum.

Angostura Cask Collection No. 1

PRODUCER: Angostura Holdings Limited

AREA OF ORIGIN: Trinidad and Tobago

VARIETY: Aged rum

ABV: 40.0%

WEBSITE: www.angostura.com

The Cask Collection is a range of limited editions entirely dedicated to rums that are matured in different types of casks. No. 1 Once Used French Oak is bottled at 40.0% and is the first rum that Angostura has matured in French oak casks. It is an exquisite, silky smooth and complex blend – created with a combination of techniques learnt from the Old World and perfected in the New World. Only 15 030 bottles of this rum were released so it may be difficult to find. A range of rums are matured for 10 years and then transferred to French Oak casks for another six years. The resulting rum is smooth and balanced with a soft silky finish.

Antiguo de Solera

PRODUCER: Santa Teresa

AREA OF ORIGIN: Estada Aragua, Venezuela

VARIETY: Dark rum

ABV: 40.0%

WEBSITE: www.ronsantateresa.com

Considered by many to be the world's best South American Rum, Antiguo de Solera is just that – an aged rum produced through a solera system, where rum is taken away for filling from the bottom of the solera, and new rum is added at the top.

The distillery is unique. It rehabilitates former gang members when they are released from prison, and gives them the means to work hard to turn their lives around – and it encourages them to play rugby, of all things.

The rum is extraordinarily complex and rounded, with notes of tobacco smoke, leather, dark chocolate and honey.

A world-class operation in all respects.

Appleton Estate 21 Year Old

PRODUCER: Gruppo Campari

AREA OF ORIGIN: Nassau Valley, Jamaica

VARIETY: Dark rum

ABV: 43.0%

WEBSITE: www.appletonestate.com

The age on a bottle of spirits can mean various things. In the case of single malt whisky, the age refers to the youngest whisky in the bottle; even one drop of a young whisky and that is its age. But other spirits have looser definitions. Appleton Estate 21 Year Old, though, adamantly follows the single malt route, and contains rums that are at least 21 years old. Most of the rum was matured and the time in the oak gives some delicious tannin spice and oaky notes. But there are some exquisite flavours of vanilla, cocoa and orange. As a result, this is a fabulous sipping rum and doesn't need mixing. It is described as 'just brilliant' by one leading online retailer.

Appleton Rare Blend 12 Year Old

PRODUCER: Gruppo Campari

AREA OF ORIGIN: Nassau Valley, Jamaica

VARIETY: Golden rum

ABV: 43.0%

WEBSITE: www.appletonestate.com

Campari spent much of the second decade of the new millennium building a portfolio of drinks businesses, and earned industry respect by taking a hands-off approach, providing the necessary funds to allow the spirits makers to do what they do best – make great drinks. Appleton, based on an estate in the heart of Jamaica, puts a big emphasis on terroir (the whole environment a drink is produced in, including weather, geography, etc.), arguing that its rums are unique due to the sugarcane that it grows itself, and the limestone spring that supplies its water. Rare Blend
12 Year Old is a blend of different rums from the estate, most of them matured in 180-litre American oak barrels. This is smooth, sweet and not as oaky as you might expect, given the age of the spirits.

Bacardi Carta Blanca

PRODUCER: Bacardi Brown Forman

AREA OF ORIGIN: Puerto Rico

VARIETY: White rum

ABV: 37.5%

WEBSITE: www3.bacardi.com

Familiarity can breed contempt but this rum is a success because of its quality. This is the world famous version of Bacardi, the one seen in tens of thousands of bars, and there are very good reasons for its global success. White rums were considered to be harsh, crude, and unrefined until they were reinvented by the company's founder, Don Facundo, who introduced charcoal filtration to remove the rum's impurities, and oak-ageing to smooth the raw edges of the spirit and produce a mellow, clear, white rum. This is a perfectly good rum, but it is deliberately smooth and unchallenging – and this might not appeal to serious rum drinkers.

Bacardi Gran Reserva Maestro de Ron

PRODUCER: Bacardi Brown Forman

AREA OF ORIGIN: Puerto Rico

VARIETY: Premium white rum

ABV: 40.0%

WEBSITE: www3.bacardi.com

Bacardi doesn't sit on its laurels, and over the years has launched different bottlings for different audiences. This Gran Reserva is a brave and confident take on super premium rum, and is an attempt to encourage rum to be sipped. Launched into travel retail, it has been well received. It is said to be inspired by a recipe passed down through generations of master blenders using a slow-filtering of the blended rum – aged up to three years – through a coconut shell charcoal, creating a smooth rum. The colour from this process has been stripped out, and presumably some of the flavour has, but this is still great: fruity, floral, and with vanilla notes and hints of walnut, oak and almond. Overall it is mellow, with slightly sweet notes.

Bacardi Superior Ron Heritage

PRODUCER: Bacardi Brown Forman

AREA OF ORIGIN: Puerto Rico

VARIETY: Premium white rum

ABV: 44.5%

WEBSITE: www3.bacardi.com

This is a very limited expression of Bacardi, with only 7,500 cases being released in 2009. It marks the 100th anniversary of the arrival of the Daiquiri in America. The cocktail was created in Cuba using Bacardi as its base, as the company was still based there in 1909. This is said to be a recreation of the original Bacardi, and it comes in a replica of the original bottle from that time. The rum itself is a richer, fuller rum than Bacardi's current standard rum, and is bottled at the same strength as it was in 1909. This is a tasty rum that can be drunk over ice. You'll find cinnamon and other spices, baked apple and sweet pear.

Basseterre Guadeloupe 1995

PRODUCER: Montebello / Carrère

AREA OF ORIGIN: Basse-Terre, Guadeloupe

VARIETY: Dark rum

ABV: 58.2%

WEBSITE: www.facebook.com/RhumMontebello

Guadeloupe has several respected rum distillers and this one – called Carrère but better known as Montebello – is one of the best. It was founded in 1930 and has been thriving ever since. With about 25 employees, it is not a small distillery, but all of the fermentation, distillation, ageing, and bottling is done under the close supervision of the Marsolle family. The estate has only 15 hectares of cane today, so most of the year-old cane is bought from farmers in the Petit-Bourg area. Beautifully packaged and very much at the premium end of the rum market, Basseterre Guadeloupe was distilled at Montebello in 1995. A blend of agricole and molasses rums bottled at cask strength, this has notes of cumin, liquorice and lemon.

Bayou Silver

PRODUCER: Bayou Rum Distillery

AREA OF ORIGIN: Lacassine, Louisiana, USA

VARIETY: White rum

ABV: 40.0%

WEBSITE: www.bayourum.com

Bayou Rum's approach to making rum is to take the finest local ingredients, distill traditionally, and innovate as it sees fit. All of Bayou's rum is handmade using traditional methods with state-of-the-art technology for all four steps: fermentation, distillation, maturation, and bottling. Distillation is carried out in traditional pot stills. But the distillery is not afraid to branch out into new and unusual areas. It makes a premium rum liqueur using locally sourced satsumas, for instance. Bayou Silver is the distillery's flagship rum, a white rum. It is not a conventional rum at all: it is a creamy flavoursome spirit with orange notes, and a sharp alcohol bite, not unlike tequila.

Bayou Spiced

PRODUCER: Bayou Rum Distillery

AREA OF ORIGIN: Lacassine, Louisiana, USA

VARIETY: Spiced rum

ABV: 40.0%

WEBSITE: www.bayourum.com

On the face of it, the idea of a rum made in the bayous of Louisiana would seem to be a strange one. Ponder it a bit longer, though, and it makes total sense. Sugarcane has been cultivated in the state since the 1700s, but no one had harnessed this abundant natural resource to create a top-notch, premium rum. So three childhood friends decided to do something about it. They set up a distillery to produce Bayou Rum in 2013 and since then have won scores of awards, and their distillery has become the largest privately-owned rum distillery in the United States. This spiced version has all the classic rum spices but the distillers have added some local ingredients to give it a Louisiana twist. A stylish spirit.

Blackwell Black Gold

PRODUCER: Gruppo Campari

AREA OF ORIGIN: Jamaica

VARIETY: Dark rum

ABV: 40.0%

WEBSITE: www.blackwellrum.com

What does this rum have in common with Roxy music, reggae and Free? The answer is Chris Blackwell who, among other things, founded Island Records and the Island Outpost resorts group. He was born and raised in Jamaica and his mother's family once owned Wray & Nephew. Wray & Nephew (owned by Gruppo Campari) make and bottle Blackwell Black Gold, named after Chris Blackwell, on its Appleton Estate in Jamaica. Appleton has a distinctive distillation process that sets its rums apart, and Black Gold is a dark rum made up of a blend of pot and column still rums. This is an exotic rum, with a tropical fruit and toffee nose and an oaky and fruity palate, with some nuttiness, treacle, and coffee. An excellent cocktail rum.

Bombo Caramel & Coconut

PRODUCER: The Real Rum Company

AREA OF ORIGIN: Newquay, Cornwall

VARIETY: Flavoured rum

ABV: 40.0%

WEBSITE: www.bomborum.com

With the moniker 'the drink of pirates', the announcement on the website that the company was conceived in Cornish pub The Limpetts Arms, and a team that includes Captain Jack The Rack, Jack the VAT as ship's accountant, and Jack the Slap as the 'ship's jailer,' Cornwall's The Real Rum Company is out for some fun with the rum category. According to the company, Bombo is a style of rum originating from an 18th-century pirate recipe in which rum was mixed with sugar and spices. The company has three flavoured rums, which are blends of golden rum with caramel, spices and fruit. In this rum the coconut is to the fore, giving a distinctly Caribbean feel to the sweet core rum.

Brugal Anejo

PRODUCER: Edrington Group

AREA OF ORIGIN: Dominican Republic

VARIETY: Dark rum

ABV: 38.0%

WEBSITE: www.brugal-rum.com

Brugal is a family company founded in 1888 by Don Andrés Brugal Montaner, and it is now run by the fifth generation of the Brugal family. Brugal Anejo is the family's original rum and Anejo means 'aged' in the case of tequila or rum, which means a spirit aged for between one and seven years, normally in an oak barrel. This rum is from the Dominican Republic and it has been matured in American ex-bourbon casks for up to five years. But the smooth taste is due to the removal of heavier alcohols during distillation, and this is considered a premium rum because of its rounded, smooth mouthfeel and taste.

Bundaberg Overproof

PRODUCER: Bundaberg Distillery

AREA OF ORIGIN: Bundaberg, Australia

VARIETY: Gold rum

ABV: 57.7%

WEBSITE: www.bundabergrum.com.au

Everyone in Australia knows Bundaberg. It comes in a distinctive square bottle with a white bear as its logo, and it's something of a national institution Down Under. The distillery, which is in Queensland, has a history stretching back to the 1880s, and its rums have a fine reputation for quality. This overproof version is produced in a similar way to the standard version but on a much smaller scale. There are many similar taste characteristics too, but the extra ageing and the added alcohol strength helps to make Overproof a fruitier, easy drinking and rounded rum with extra intensity and bite.

Bundaberg Rum Solera

PRODUCER: Bundaberg Distillery

AREA OF ORIGIN: Bundaberg, Australia

VARIETY: Dark rum

ABV: 40.0%

WEBSITE: www.bundabergrum.com.au

When a group of Queenslanders decided that there was a better use for sugarcane than making cakes, Bundaberg was born. Rum was already popular in Australia but Bundaberg quickly established itself in Western Australia, Sydney and Melbourne.

Bundaberg's Rum Solera is considered by the distillery as its masterpiece, and it is not alone in holding this opinion. This rum was chosen as the world's best dark rum in the 2017 World Drink Awards in London.

'This is our finest and most intricate rum and testament to our unwavering search for true perfection in craftsmanship,' say the distillers. 'The complex solera process begins with our finest aged dark rum reserves, carefully matured in selected rich port, full-bodied bourbon and sweet sherry barrels.'

Caña Brava Anejo

PRODUCER: Las Cabres

AREA OF ORIGIN: Herrera, Panama

VARIETY: Golden rum

ABV: 45.0%

WEBSITE: www.canabravarum.com

Las Cabres distillery was established in 1919 but it was with the arrival of Francisco 'Don Pancho' J. Fernandez that the distillery joined the world's elite rum making facilities. Don Pancho had made rum in his native Cuba for more than 35 years, employing the feted 'Cuban method' of production, before moving to Panama in the early 1990s, bringing his expertise with him.

In the mid-1990s, Don Pancho and Carlos Esquivel uncovered a copper column still in an abandoned warehouse, with a small medallion inscribed 'Cincinnati 1922'. He used the still, along with his own skills and experience, to produce the Caña Brava range. This particular rum is aged for seven years in ex-bourbon and Tennessee whiskey barrels. There are some tropical fruit notes on the palate.

Captain Bligh XO

PRODUCER: St Vincent Distillers Ltd

AREA OF ORIGIN: Saint Vincent and The Grenadines

VARIETY: Gold rum

ABV: 40.0%

WEBSITE: www.sunsetrum.com

The story of Captain William Bligh, the mutiny on his ship *The Bounty*, and how he and his banished crew navigated their way to survival, is well known. And while that should be enough for anyone, Captain Bligh faced another major incident in his life. Fifteen years after the mutiny he was appointed governor of New South Wales, and his principle job was to clean up the corrupt rum trade there. But his actions against the New South Wales Corps led to a rebellion and he was deposed – the only time in Australian history that an armed rebellion successfully overthrew a government. Captain Bligh XO is an award-winning and easy drinking rum that has been matured in ex-bourbon barrels for about a decade. The taste balances vanilla and oak, and has a pleasant coconut aftertaste.

Captain Morgan Original

PRODUCER: Diageo

AREA OF ORIGIN: Jamaica, Guyana, Barbados

VARIETY: Dark rum

ABV: 40.0%

WEBSITE: www.captainmorgan.com

Captain Morgan is one of rum's most famous brands, but familiarity shouldn't breed contempt. This blend of various Caribbean rums has been made with the same love and attention to detail as the best blended Scotch whisky. Captain Morgan is named after Sir Henry Morgan, a Welsh buccaneer or 'legal' pirate, given the freedom to terrorise and plunder the ships of rival nations (he later became Governor of Jamaica). The story goes that after a successful outing the crew would party hard in taverns across the Caribbean, drinking rum. This rum is designed to revive those parties. It's a pleasant, easy drinking, and very mixable rum, which has rightly enjoyed huge popularity for decades. It contains a mix of pot still and continuous still rums.

Captain
Morgan

IMPORTED

Captain Morgan

JAMAICA RUM

IMPORTED

DISTILLED IN JAMAICA UNDER
GOVERNMENT SUPERVISION

750ml   40% vol.

MATURED AND BOTTLED IN THE U.K.

PRODUCED BY CAPTAIN MORGAN RUM CO.

Captain Morgan Original Spiced Gold

PRODUCER: Diageo

AREA OF ORIGIN: Jamaica, Guyana, Barbados

VARIETY: Spiced rum

ABV: 35.0%

WEBSITE: www.captainmorgan.com

It's hard to take a rum seriously when the marketing folk behind it paid a lot of money to Leicester City football captain Wes Morgan to dress up as Captain Morgan and go to bars shouting 'I'm Captain Morgan!', before handing out free drinks. But this is a seriously good spiced rum, a secret mix of spirit, spice and natural flavours matured in charred oak barrels. It's such a good rum that it has become the flagship expression for Captain Morgan. It is best served in a tankard over ice, with cola and a slice of lime. The producers describe the rum as rich, with natural vanilla, brown sugar, dried fruit, and warming spices with hints of oak.

ORIGINAL
The **SPICED GOLD**

Clément Rhum Agricole Select Barrel

PRODUCER: Clément

AREA OF ORIGIN: Le François, Martinique

VARIETY: Rhum agricole

ABV: 40.0%

WEBSITE: www.rhum-clement.com/en

1887 saw the peak of a sugar crisis. The introduction of sugar beets and the increasing availability of cheap South American sugar led to the collapse of the Martiniquean sugar industry. At this time Homère Clément purchased the Domaine de l'Acajou sugar plantation and transformed it into a producer of world-class rhum agricole. Homère mimicked the distillers of the great Armagnacs to perfect his method of rum production, known today as rhum agricole. Clément Select Barrel is a contemporary style of rhum agricole crafted with a blend of rums matured in selected barrels with a particularly heavy toasting. It is soft and rounded with a mix of spice box aromas, and gentle vanilla bean on the finish.

Clément XO

PRODUCER: Clément

AREA OF ORIGIN: Le François, Martinique

VARIETY: Rhum agricole

ABV: 44.0%

WEBSITE: www.rhum-clement.com/en

Clément is a company originally established in the early part of the 20th century by Homère Clément, physician and mayor of Le François. He purchased the prestigious 43-hectare sugar plantation Domaine de L'Acajou, and pioneered rhum agricole, a contemporary style of pure rum made directly from fresh free-run sugarcane juice, instead of the traditional rum made from molasses. Since the early days the company has built a reputation for fine rum. This XO is released every year, and features carefully selected aged rhum agricole, aged for a minimum of six years in a combination of virgin and re-charred oak barrels. This rum is accentuated by the intense charred wood flavours balanced by the natural sweetness of the sugarcane distillate, and has floral notes.

Cloven Hoof

PRODUCER: Guilty Libations

AREA OF ORIGIN: Oxford, England

VARIETY: Spiced rum

ABV: 37.5%

WEBSITE: www.clovenhoofrum.com

Cloven Hoof is to rum what Monkey Shoulder is to whisky: fun and irreverent on the outside, and a pretty cool spirit within. Forsaking bad cartoon piracy and imagery, the producers of this rum have gone down a more diabolical route. The company's mission statement says it is anti-corporate and people-facing, and there is a rich vein of fun in its make up. Nevertheless, this is still a serious rum. It contains spirit imported from Guyana's Diamond Distillery, and a rum from Trinidad that has a distinctive cough candy smell and taste. In England cloves and natural spices are added to create an intriguing but highly palatable rum. Cloven Hoof is sold across the South of England, and is hoping to widen distribution in time.

Cruzan Single Barrel

PRODUCER: The Nelthropp Family

AREA OF ORIGIN: St Croix, US Virgin Islands

VARIETY: Golden rum

ABV: 40.0%

WEBSITE: www.cruzanrum.com

Since the early 1800s, the Nelthropp Family has called St. Croix home, and they have become an integral part of the island's history. For the last 200 years, the island has not only left its mark on the Nelthropps, but also on their rum. The family say the unique character of St Croix is echoed in every bottle of Cruzan rum, from distilling perfected on the island over generations, to the warm, tropical breezes that circulate through the open-air warehouses of the distillery. Even the name reflects the people of St Croix, who are known as Crucians. Cruzan Single Barrel is made with rums aged for up to 12 years, which are blended and allowed to marry for a further year in new charred oak barrels. So not technically a single barrel bottling at all – but fine rum nevertheless.

Dark Matter Spiced

PRODUCER: Dark Matter Distillers

AREA OF ORIGIN: Banchory, Scotland

VARIETY: Spiced rum

ABV: 40.0%

WEBSITE: www.darkmatterdistillers.com

Dark Matter Distillery sprung from a grain of an idea sparked by the refusal of three Dominican Republic rum distilleries to let holidaymaker Jim Ewen visit them, prompting him to remark that it would be easier to build his own distillery.

The former petroleum economist teamed up with his brother, John, overcame investment issues and built Scotland's first purpose-built rum distillery. They took two years to come up with their unique take on a spiced rum, which includes fresh ginger, green peppercorns and dried long pepper.

'The taste equivalent of warping into a liquid black hole but without every atom in your body being crushed to an infinitely small point,' says the distillery. Nicely put, guys.

Dark Matter

MOLECULAR ENGINEERING
SCOTLAND

LOGIC

OUR CURIOSITY DRIVES US
WHILE SCIENCE INSPIRES
US. COMBINING KNOWLEDGE
AND IMAGINATION WE
OBSESSIVELY PURSUE
FLAVOUR THROUGH
SYSTEMATIC STUDY,
OBSERVATION AND
EXPERIMENT.

SPICED RUM

700ml℮

ALCOHOL VOLUME
40%

Dead Man's Fingers Cornish Spiced Rum

PRODUCER: The Rum & Crab Shack

AREA OF ORIGIN: St Ives, Cornwall

VARIETY: Spiced rum

ABV: 37.5%

WEBSITE: deadmansfingers.com

Whoever came up with the idea of combining top quality rums with local crab and other Cornish and Dorset seafood is a genius; and launching their own spiced rum was very smart indeed. St Ives is one of two Rum and Crab Shacks, offering a taste of the sea from both sides of the Atlantic. Both sites offer a good selection of rum, but the owners created Dead Man's Fingers to bring a taste of Cornwall to Caribbean rum. This is a delicious spiced rum and you'll find flavours of saffron, caramel, vanilla, cinnamon, nutmeg and orange. Available by the nip at the Rum & Crab shack, and by the bottle from several online retailers.

Dictador 12 Year Old

PRODUCER: Dictador

AREA OF ORIGIN: Colombia

VARIETY: Dark rum

ABV: 40.0%

WEBSITE: www.dictador.com

Bottle age can be a source of confusion. A Cognac expert recently introduced a Cognac as a 60 year-old because it had been matured for 10 years in cask and then bottled 50 years ago. In Scotland if that was a single malt it would still be 10 years old. Rum often isn't fussy how it approaches age, so there's this: this is an average, and includes rums from eight to 14 years old. It is different for two reasons: firstly, it is made using a solera system, with younger rums being added at the top to older rums lower down, softening the overall palate feel. Secondly, the rum is not made from molasses but from sugarcane honey. Molasses are in short supply in Colombia because they are used to make biofuel. The resulting rum is complex and excellent, with a delicate smokiness, okay tannins and some attractive fruity notes.

Diplomático Reserva Exclusiva

PRODUCER: Diplomático

AREA OF ORIGIN: Venezuela

VARIETY: Gold rum

ABV: 40.0%

WEBSITE: rondiplomatico.com

Diplomático has had a chequered history but it's enough to know that it was bought by a group of Venezuelan entrepreneurs in the 1950s and has gone from strength to strength despite the country's political difficulties in recent years. The distillery is sited at the start of the Andes, close to the sugarcane-producing regions and a pure water source. Everything about this rum exudes quality. It is an elegant and complex sipping rum, crafted from pure sugarcane honeys. It is distilled slowly on old copper pot stills and aged in small ex-whisky oak casks for up to 12 years. The result is a classy, fruity, full-bodied rum that is fine served neat for sipping.

Don Q 151° Rum

PRODUCER: Serrallés family

AREA OF ORIGIN: Ponce, Puerto Rico

VARIETY: Golden rum

ABV: 75.5%

WEBSITE: www.donq.com

Don Q is made at the Serrallés distillery, which is named after founder Don Juan Serrallés, who vastly expanded the family sugarcane business and founded the Serrallés rum making tradition. Using a copper pot still he imported from France, he produced the first casks of rum sold under the Serrallés name. Since then the company has passed through the generations, as Puerto Rico's reputation for quality rum has grown. The 151° refers to the proof strength, a whopping 75.5% ABV, but this is regarded as one of the smoothest over-proof rums and it is a great base for cocktails. It has dark coffee, banana, and spicy oak notes, as well as some smoky tobacco notes.

Don Q Reserva De La Familia Serrallés

PRODUCER: Serrallés Family

AREA OF ORIGIN: Ponce, Puerto Rico

VARIETY: Aged rum

ABV: 40.0%

WEBSITE: www.donq.com

This has been described as the most exclusive rum in the world, and it's another one that is most likely to be found in the secondary market rather than at a High Street retailer. This distillery is best known for making Don Q rum and this very limited special edition was released to celebrate Don Q's 150th anniversary. It is a blend but contains rums distilled in 1994 and aged in charred American-oak barrels for 20 years. After the rums were combined the blend was returned to the charred barrels for a few months so a balance between aroma and taste could be achieved. The bottle is presented in a luxury glass decanter with accompanying three-piece, solid-wood box.

Dunedin Rum

PRODUCER: Strathearn Distillery

AREA OF ORIGIN: Methven, Scotland

VARIETY: Golden rum

ABV: 43.0%

WEBSITE: www.strathearndistillery.com

Strathearn may well be Scotland's smallest distillery, and it is one of a number of new draft distilleries. In 2017 Strathearn started bottling its single cask single malt whiskies, with the first bottle fetching £4150 at auction, and the rest of the cask selling at between £325 and £525 a bottle. This rum is one of a number of spirits released to fill the gap while waiting for the whisky to mature. This is a golden rum, probably the first made in Scotland for more than 100 years. It has a pleasant wave of spices and toasted oak as well as the more common vanilla and burnt sugar notes.

El Dorado 12 Year Old

PRODUCER: Demerara Distillers Ltd

AREA OF ORIGIN: Guyana

VARIETY: Gold rum

ABV: 40.0%

WEBSITE: theeldoradorum.com

El Dorado is, of course, the legendary and fabled city made of gold, supposedly hidden away in the heart of Guyana. But while El Dorado the golden city doesn't exist, a range of rums bearing its name does. Each of the company's rums is made at the Demerara Distillery, which has nine stills. This 12 year is labelled in the same way as malt whisky, so all the spirit is at least 12 years old, and is a blend of pot still and coffey still rums. This is a highly respected rum, which has won a large number of awards. Expect to find juicy raisins, cocoa, toffee, vanilla and spice on the palate.

El Dorado 25 Year Old Grand Special Reserve

PRODUCER: Demerara Distillers Ltd

AREA OF ORIGIN: Demerara, Guyana

VARIETY: Aged rum

ABV: 43.0%

WEBSITE: www.theeldoradorum.com

Demerara Distilleries Ltd is made up of several distilleries that merged and eventually ended up on one estate, which is called Diamond. All the stills and equipment are now based in one distillery. The El Dorado range of rums was launched in 1992 and became a tremendous success locally and in international markets. The 25-year-old expression is a very limited edition vintage rum that possesses a silky smoothness to challenge the oldest cognac. The constant ambient warmth and tropical conditions of Demerara dramatically hasten the maturation process – producing a spirit that is the equivalent of one aged for many more years in a cooler climate. The distillery describes this rum as rich, smooth and mellow, with soft syrupy mouthfeel and subtle notes of caramel and heavy fruit cake.

Elements 8 Barrel Infused Spiced Rum

PRODUCER: Elements 8

AREA OF ORIGIN: St Lucia

VARIETY: Spiced rum

ABV: 40.0%

WEBSITE: www.mangroveuk.com/elements-8-rum

This rum means business. It is made to the highest standards and has built up a worldwide cult following. The producer's name reflects the eight elements used in the production of rum. Elements 8 is distilled and aged in the oldest distillery in St Lucia, which has more than 120 years of rum-making experience. It is a complex 'hand blend' of over 10 different types of rum, and is distilled using three artisan distillation techniques. It is fermented with three unique yeast strains to give it a complex depth. This is made up of top quality St Lucia dark rum and includes 10 exotic fruits and spices, including clove, cinnamon, vanilla, ginger, nutmeg, star anise, coconut, orange, lemon and honey.

Flor de Caña 12 Years

PRODUCER: Compañia de Licorera

AREA OF ORIGIN: Managua, Nicaragua

VARIETY: Dark rum

ABV: 40.0%

WEBSITE: www.flordecana.com

Flor de Caña is produced in Managua by a company with its roots going back to the 19th century, though this range of rums was introduced in the 1990s. The company makes both white and dark rums and has established a reputation for well crafted and outstanding rums. The rums are matured in former bourbon white oak casks, so oaky tannin notes are present, as well as toffee and vanilla from the wood. What sets this rum apart is the delightful apple note that is present in the taste. Few spirits drinks have won as many awards internationally as this one.

Foursquare Port Cask Finish

PRODUCER: Foursquare Distillery

AREA OF ORIGIN: St Philip, Barbados

VARIETY: Aged rum

ABV: 40.0%

Foursquare Rum distillery was founded by Reginald Leon Seale, the great-great grandfather of the current master blender and distiller Richard Seale. The distillery has become a byword for classic Caribbean rum.

The Port Cask Finish is a blend of pot and column distilled rum, all of which are distilled, blended and bottled at Foursquare. The word 'Finish' implies that this rum spends only a short time in a port cask after being mainly matured in another cask. This is not the case. The rum spends three years in an ex-bourbon cask and is then transferred to a 220-litre port cask for a weighty six years. The result is a quality spiced rum with cinnamon, nutmeg, ginger and cherry menthol notes.

PRODUCT OF BARBADOS

80 PROOF

Foursquare Rum Distillery

St. Philip, Barbados

FINE BARBADOS RUM

PORT CASK FINISH

EXCEPTIONAL CASK SELECTION

Wood: Bourbon & Port

Cask Storage: 9 years

Blend No.:   162

Bottled   June 2014

Distilled, blended and bottled by R.L.Seale & Co. Ltd
Foursquare Rum Distillery, St. Philip, Barbados.

40% Alc
by Vol.

Gold of Mauritius

PRODUCER: Grays Inc Ltd

AREA OF ORIGIN: Mauritius

VARIETY: Dark rum

ABV: 40.0%

WEBSITE: www.grays.mu

A few years ago an independent Scottish whisky retailer tried to promote a range of rums in the same way as you would a malt whisky: by region. It even matched rums to malt whisky styles. It had a valid point. Mauritius has a distinctive rum style and a history stretching back to 1850. Several distilleries operate there, and its tropical climate and rich volcanic soils ensure excellent sugarcane. Every bottle of Gold of Mauritius is blended under the supervision of Frederic Bestel, who selects specific un-aged rums from local Mauritian distilleries before conditioning the rum in South African port casks. The result is a winey, distinctive rum heavily influenced by the port casks.

Gosling's Black Seal 151 Proof

PRODUCER: Gosling Brothers Limited

AREA OF ORIGIN: Bermuda

VARIETY: Dark rum

ABV: 75.5%

WEBSITE: www.goslingsrum.com

When it comes to happy accidents, they don't come much happier than that of Gosling's and Bermuda. The company has a history stretching back more than 200 years. In 1806 founder James Gosling was looking to expand his business in to America, so he set out with a small fortune and all that he needed to succeed. Three months later, after weeks of sailing on becalmed waters, he had failed to reach America. When his ship charter ran out he headed for the nearest port – St George's in Bermuda. And it was from there that he launched his successful new venture. This expression is a big, full frontal vanilla- and caramel-flavoured mixing rum.

Gosling's Family Reserve Old Rum

PRODUCER: Gosling Brothers Limited

AREA OF ORIGIN: Bermuda

VARIETY: Aged rum

ABV: 40.0%

WEBSITE: www.goslingsrum.com

Gosling is most famous for its Black Seal range, written about elsewhere in this book, but this is something of a hidden gem, and is well worth seeking out. It is the same blend as Black Seal but is aged for much longer. The result is an aged rum that bears comparison to fine brandy or single malt. The bottles are hand labelled, dipped in wax, and presented in a stylish box. But it's the taste that you'll be waxing eloquently about: it's rich, full, oaky, and with layer after layer of dried and stewed fruits. As good as sipping rum gets, and a must for rum fans.

GOSLING'S
FAMILY RESERVE RUM

Gosling's Family Reserve OLD RUM
has been a secret for generations enjoyed
only by members of the family.
OLD RUM is created from the
incomparable Bermuda blend that makes
up the smooth, full flavor of Gosling's
Black Seal Rum.
The rum is left resting in the oak barrels
where it is aged until it has acquired a
luscious, well-balanced complexity,
resulting in the finest
of sipping rums.

OLD RUM

This rich, soft, elegant OLD RUM is
created for the enjoyment of those who
appreciate the finer things in life.
Welcome to the family!

Gosling's
SINCE 1806

Bottle No. 11 6?/3/13

750ml   40% ALC/VOL

Havana Club 3

PRODUCER: Havana Club International

AREA OF ORIGIN: Havana, Cuba

VARIETY: White rum

ABV: 40.0%

WEBSITE: www.havana-club.co.uk

Towards the end of the Barack Obama presidency all eyes were on Cuba, as the possibility of an end to the trade embargo seemed to be becoming a reality. Rum would have been directly affected, and particularly this brand, which is a joint partnership between the Cuban rum industry and Pernod Ricard. Now all bets are off, as Donald Trump batons down the hatches again. Watch out for imitators – 'the real Havana Club' is not – it's an America-only me-too brand.

Havana Club 3 is a purely Cuban and authentic three-year-old white rum that bursts with character. It may be a familiar name but this is the real McCoy, as the large number of reviews on The Whisky Exchange website prove. This is quality rum, heaven-sent for making classic Cuban cocktails.

Havana Club 15 Year Old Gran Reserva

PRODUCER: Havana Club International

AREA OF ORIGIN: Havana, Cuba

VARIETY: Dark rum

ABV: 40.0%

WEBSITE: www.havana-club.co.uk

When folk argue that Cuba makes the world's best rum, the chances are they are thinking of this rum in particular. There are lots of great rums in the world but this is the rum equivalent of Highland Park 18 Year Old single malt whisky: a complete all rounder, ticking every taste box, making it an objective candidate for the ultimate spirit – and not just a subjective one. Havana Club Rum 15 Year Old Gran Reserva is created by selecting the best rums of Cuba and ageing them in a complex and lengthy way. The results are, according to The Whisky Exchange website, 'simply awesome'. This is a balanced and complete rum with plenty of oaky notes, and it warrants being savoured slowly.

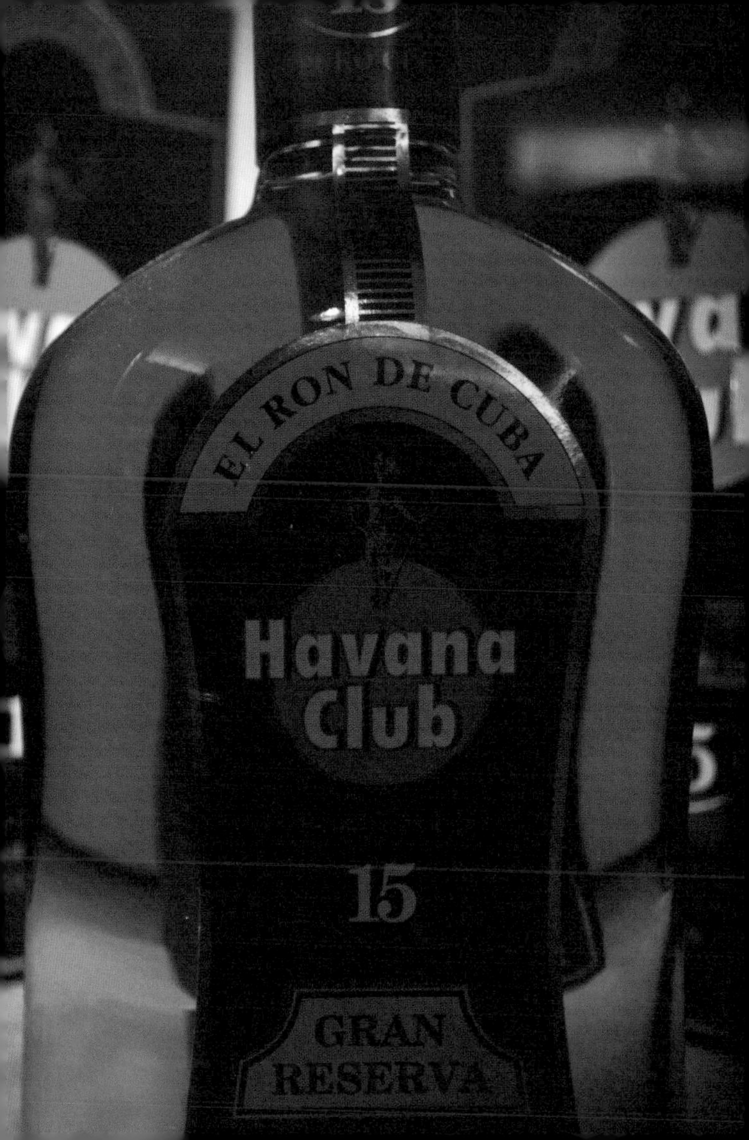
EL RON DE CUBA
Havana
Club
15
GRAN
RESERVA

Havana Club Selección de Maestros

PRODUCER: Havana Club International

AREA OF ORIGIN: Cuba

VARIETY: Dark rum

ABV: 45.0%

WEBSITE: www.havanaclub.com

To make this special rum, Havana Club, owned by Pernod Ricard, brought together all the members of the Guild de Maestros del Ron Cubano and asked them to work together. Led by the acclaimed rum maker Don José Navarro, the group first met to select the finest and most exceptional aged rums from the island. The selected rums were blended and then further aged, before the Guild members finally picked the rums that matured the best; this happens every time a batch of this rum is made. The finished rum is exceptional, with leather, cigars, orange, coffee beans, and cedar wood. Beautifully packaged, too.

HSE Rhum Élevé Sous Bois

PRODUCER: HSE

AREA OF ORIGIN: Martinique

VARIETY: Aged rum

ABV: 42.0%

WEBSITE: www.rhum-hse.com

HSE Rhum Élevé Sous Bois is another rum distilled on the French outpost island of Martinique, and the distillery has a history stretching back to the 1880s. 'sous bois' means the rum is matured in wood and this is an amber agricole rum that has been aged for a minimum of 12–18 months in large oak vats, which is a relatively short period of time. Many people go from white to three-year rum and miss out this neglected French rhum style. Shame. This has floral, fruity and vanilla aromas, and softens and smooths out the distinct sugarcane edges found in white rum. It's very elegant and dignified, with notes of raisin, white grape juice, pears and vanilla. It can be hard to find.

Inner Circle Green Dot

PRODUCER: Vok Beverages

AREA OF ORIGIN: Salisbury South, Australia

VARIETY: Golden rum

ABV: 57.2%

WEBSITE: www.vok.com.au

This Australian rum is called Inner Circle because originally it was made available only to the board of directors of Australia's Colonial Sugar Refining Company and a handful of its prized clients. But despite the exclusivity, its reputation for outstanding flavour spread. The brand was sold on and eventually ended up with Vok Beverages, a company established in 2002 as an independently owned and operated alcohol company. It is one of Australia's fastest growing beverage companies. Inner Circle is now totally Australian owned and operated. This rum is made with Fijian sugarcane, grown using traditional harvesting techniques. Despite its high strength the flavours hold up well, and it is surprisingly rounded and smooth.

Island Company Rum

PRODUCER: Island Company

AREA OF ORIGIN: West Palm Beach, USA

VARIETY: Golden rum

ABV: 40.0%

WEBSITE: www.islandcompanyrum.com

With the tagline 'simply the smoothest', the makers of Island Company Rum aim high, and that's not surprising when you consider the company behind the brand. Island Company targets high-end retailers in luxury five-star resorts – it started life as a small bikini-making business but is now the supplier of a diverse range of beach-linked clothing, swimwear, resort wear, sun care, and accessories. There is some logic in extending the company's interests to rum. The rum comes from Trinidad and is distilled five times. Because they're cool and trendy, the company points out that this rum is gluten-, sugar- and carb-free.

ISLAND COMPANY

RUM

SIMPLY THE SMOOTHEST

FIVE TIMES DISTILLED

ZERO CARBS
GLUTEN FREE

40% ALC/VOL (80 PROOF)

PRODUCT OF TRINIDAD

750 ML.

Kill Devil Irma, Shipwreck Series

PRODUCER: Outer Banks Distilling

AREA OF ORIGIN: Manteo, USA

VARIETY: Aged rum

ABV: 40.0%

WEBSITE: www.outerbanksdistilling.com

Kill Devil Irma is the first in a series of releases by Kill Devil, called Shipwreck. Irma was the name of a three-masted schooner that was wrecked along the beach in Kill Devil Hills in 1925, in front of the Croatan Inn.

Each release is a small batch rum, aged in unique barrels crafted from a variety of ingredients. Different styles of molasses, sugars and barrels are used to highlight the versatility of the spirit for each offering in this series. For batch one, a blend of molasses and Demerara sugar was used to complement flavours derived from ageing in four 10-gallon (45-litre) barrels from Tuthilltown Spirits in New York – two ex-bourbon, two ex-rye.

Kill Devil Pecan Rum

PRODUCER: Outer Banks Distilling

AREA OF ORIGIN: Manteo, USA

VARIETY: Aged rum

ABV: 40.0%

WEBSITE: www.outerbanksdistilling.com

Kill Devil is an American rum company set up by a group of friends with a love of brewing beer and drinking rum. The name of the rum, and the company, is dripping in history and heritage. Kill Devil is an original name for rum, and it probably reached the American coastline on ships smashed up off the Outer Banks – known as the 'graveyard of the Atlantic' because it has witnessed more than 1000 wrecks. The distillery operates close to Kill Devil Hills, probably named after the casks of rum washed up on the shore. This smooth, nutty and sweet rum is flavoured with honey from a neighbouring town, and from locally produced pecans.

Koko Kanu Coconut

PRODUCER: Gruppo Campari

AREA OF ORIGIN: Kingston, Jamaica

VARIETY: Flavoured white rum

ABV: 37.5%

WEBSITE: www.kokokanu.com

A fair number of the rums in this book are metaphorical elder statesmen, keen to stress their gravitas and with a burning desire to be taken seriously, not just in the rum world but in the world of spirits more generally. Koko Kanu can lay out its credentials to some degree because it's made at the Wray & Nephew distillery in Jamaica. Jamaican white rum is noted for its big flavours, and this rum is mixed with fresh coconut essence. There are none of the artificial flavours that sometimes mar flavoured spirits of this nature. It tastes great, is a flexible party drink, and can be consumed neat or as a mixer, and goes well with fruit juices.

Kraken Black Spiced Rum

PRODUCER: Proximo Spirits

AREA OF ORIGIN: Jersey City, USA

VARIETY: Black spiced rum

ABV: 40.0%

WEBSITE: www.krakenrum.com

The kraken is a mythical sea beast, thought to be a giant squid, that destroyed scores of ships over the decades. The story goes that a ship carrying one of the largest quantities of black spiced rum ever to be brought over from the Caribbean islands, for unexplained reasons, never reached its destination. Legend has it that the ship was destroyed by the kraken, but casks of the black spiced rum came to shore and were renamed 'kraken'. This rum is a reproduction of that spirit. Good story, but what about the rum? It's a good quality spirit with espresso coffee, toffee and cloves, cinnamon, pepper and ginger in the spice mix.

La Hechicera Fine Aged

PRODUCER: Riascos family

AREA OF ORIGIN: Barranquilla, Colombia

VARIETY: Aged rum

ABV: 40.0%

WEBSITE: www.lahechicera.co

The Riascos family have built up an enviable reputation for creating fine rums in Colombia, over two decades and three generations. The family, travelling around the Caribbean sourcing the finest raw spirits, finding the richest casks, attracting the most talented master blenders, has created a signature style and outstanding rums.

The family owns an unassuming little bodega at the heart of Barranquilla, nestled between the long-winding Magdalena River and the Caribbean Sea. Fine Aged is a rum made using the solera method, and the spirit is aged between 12 and 21 years in ex-bourbon barrels. You can taste the quality here – there are plummy jam notes, dark coffee, a touch of pepper spice, and a pleasant oakiness. Very good indeed.

Lamb's Navy Rum

PRODUCER: Corby / Pernod Ricard

AREA OF ORIGIN: London, England

VARIETY: Golden rum

ABV: 40.0%

WEBSITE: www.lambsnavyrum.com

Lamb's Navy is one of those products that seems to have always been there, and that's because it has. It has its roots in the centuries-old link between rum and the Royal Navy, and if you want a brand that demonstrates how a rum made in a variety of West Indian islands can become such a distinctly British spirit, then this is it. It was first blended in 1849 by Alfred Lamb, who brought together 18 rums from Barbados, Trinidad and Tobago, Jamaica and Guyana. It has floated in and out of fashion ever since, but has always been a reliable, quality, value-for-money naval-style rum.

Liverpool Rum

PRODUCER: Halewood International

AREA OF ORIGIN: Liverpool, England

VARIETY: Dark rum

ABV: 43.0%

WEBSITE: www.halewood-int.com

Halewood International has been accumulating a sizeable drinks portfolio of quality British gins and vodkas. It owns Pogues Irish Whiskey, the official whiskey of the famous band of the same name, it owns renowned ginger beer and ale brand Crabbie's, and it owns the Liverpool Distillery, where this rum spends time 'resting' after being distilled in Trinidad. Liverpool Rum is a premium and rare dark rum that has been aged for 16 years. Column still produced from sugarcane molasses, the rum is subject to a double maturation period, and finished in ex-American bourbon barrels. Liverpool Rum is described as velvety smooth with a rich oaky sweetness and very subtle, elegant spice notes.

Mezan 2004 Panama

PRODUCER: Marussia Beverages

AREA OF ORIGIN: London, England

VARIETY: Golden rum

ABV: 40.0%

WEBSITE: www.mezanrum.com

Mezan specialise in single cask rums sourced from across the West Indies and Central and South America. Each rum is crafted from a single year's distillation by a single distillery. Some of the distilleries are old and traditional, others are state-of-the-art, but they are all chosen for the quality of rum they produce. Each rum is matured under close supervision, but they are otherwise untouched – that is unblended, unsweetened, uncoloured, and only lightly filtered.

This spirit from Panama is distinctive and soft and is produced in modern multi-column stills from estate-grown sugarcane. The distillery was rebuilt in 1976 and grows its own yeast, adding to the rum's individuality and character.

Mocambo 10 Year Old

PRODUCER: Licores Veracruz

AREA OF ORIGIN: Cordoba, Mexico

VARIETY: Dark rum

ABV: 40.0%

WEBSITE: www.licoresveracruz.com

You don't expect rum from a country that specialises in big, earthy, spicy and difficult spirits such as tequila and mezcal, but that's what this is: Mexican rum. Perhaps this shouldn't come as such a surprise. Licores Veracruz is sited near the coast in Cordoba and the Veracruz region has had quality sugarcane since it was introduced by the Spanish Conquistadores in the middle of the 16th century. This company makes a range of different spirits and Mocambo 10 Year Old is one of its stronger ones. It is made up of 70% rum from sugarcane juice, and 30% rum from molasses. Throw in a lengthy maturation period and you end up with a rum that is full-bodied and bold, with tobacco, green and orange fruit, and some spiciness.

Morton's OVD Demerara

PRODUCER: William Grant & Sons

AREA OF ORIGIN: Guyana

VARIETY: Dark rum

ABV: 40.0%

WEBSITE: www.ovdrum.co.uk

The history of trading makes fascinating reading. The famous spice routes and the East India Company tell many stories, and trading across the world was well and truly established by the 18th century, though it obviously had its sinister and repulsive side when it came to the Transatlantic trade triangle. Among the importers and bottlers of the 19th century was George Morton, who began importing this rum from Guyana in 1838. OVD stands for Old Vatted Demerara, and Demerara has become synonymous with sweeter rums. Perhaps that's why this one became highly successful in Scotland, a nation with a sweet tooth. It is matured in oak casks, and has a rich, creamy taste, with complex toffee notes and a mellow finish.

Mount Gay Black Barrel

PRODUCER: Remy Cointreau

AREA OF ORIGIN: Barbados

VARIETY: Dark rum

ABV: 43.0%

WEBSITE: www.mountgayrum.com

Mount Gay is another heavyweight name from the world of rum, and one with even more history and heritage than its competitors. It has a history that dates back to 1703 and although it is now owned by an international drinks company, it is the oldest continuously functioning rum distillery in the world. Barbados was one of the first islands to make rum, and it was one of the first to start producing a superior version of it. And it's to Mount Gay's credit that it is still successful and at the vanguard of a rum revival. Black Barrel was released in 2014 and is a rich, flavoured rum due to its high proportion of single column and double pot distilled rum, and maturation in heavily charred ex-bourbon barrels.

Mount Gay Eclipse

PRODUCER: Remy Cointreau

AREA OF ORIGIN: Barbados

VARIETY: Dark rum

ABV: 43.0%

WEBSITE: www.mountgayrum.com

Mount Gay is named after John Gay, who was a respected leader and businessman who dedicated his life to Barbados. He happened to have a friend, amusingly called John Sober, who inherited a then-unknown distillery and called on John Gay's help. The result was the production of a particularly good quality rum.

Mount Gay Eclipse was released to celebrate the double event in 1910 of a total eclipse of the moon and the passage of Halley's Comet. This rum has a delightful floral and honey nose and a fruity, tropical and toasted nut taste, with enough spice to stop it becoming too sweet and sickly. Very good value.

Mutineers Gold XO Special Reserve

PRODUCER: St Vincent Distillers

AREA OF ORIGIN: Kingstown, St Vincent

VARIETY: Gold rum

ABV: 40.0%

WEBSITE: www.sunsetrum.com

St Vincent Distillers distills a number of rums, including the award-winning and flagship rum, Sunset. Today, St Vincent Distillers boasts a clean, modern facility comprising an expert team of distillers, blenders, bottlers and technicians. The distillery produces rums of all styles, including white and aged rums. Mutineers Gold is an export rum distilled in the lush foothills of the Souriere volcano. It's matured in oak casks. Mutineers Gold has won a number of awards, including the 2017 Best Gold Rum at The World Rum Awards. The rum stands apart because it has a mellow, fruity and drying taste, making it very more-ish.

Myers's Rum

PRODUCER: Diageo

AREA OF ORIGIN: Jamaica

VARIETY: Dark rum

ABV: 40.0%

WEBSITE: www.diageo.com

Ah, don't you just love the smell of hyperbole in the morning?

Myers's Rum has supposedly been described by spirits retailers as the ultimate and pre-eminent cocktail dark rum, though that smells an awful lot like marketing hype. That said, it is owned by the drinks giant Diageo, and is found in stylish bars across the world. The company has stayed true to the rum, both in terms of the contents, which were created by Fred L Myers in 1879, and in terms of the packaging. It has kept its original bottle shape and tagline, 'world famous, dark and mellow' for several decades. Myers's is a blend of nine Jamaican rums aged for six years in white oak barrels. The rum has a smoky tobacco nose and a smooth spicy sweet taste.

New Grove Dark Rum

PRODUCER: Grays Distillery

AREA OF ORIGIN: Mauritius

VARIETY: Dark rum

ABV: 37.5%

WEBSITE: www.newgrove.mu

Another outstanding rum from the island of Mauritius, this time from New Grove, a small, family craft distiller. New Grove has been making premium rum since before the middle of the 19th century, using local ingredients. Its range includes aged and higher strength rums, and rums matured in unusual wood. This is one of its more conservative offerings, but it is excellent. It's made using an old family recipe and is both smooth and spicy. There are soft notes of burnt molasses too, and it's very rich and fruity. Sipping rums are becoming popular in some regions, and this fits the bill perfectly. A rum for warm summer evenings.

New Grove Old Tradition Rum

PRODUCER: Grays Inc Ltd

AREA OF ORIGIN: Pamplemousses, Mauritius

VARIETY: Aged rum

ABV: 40.0%

WEBSITE: www.newgrove.mu

New Grove is a family-run business that has been making rum on the island of Mauritius since 1852, when Dr Charles François Harel developed rum distillation there. The family had already established a sugarcane business in 1838. This five-year-old rum is described as 'full bodied' and has the words 'Old Tradition' in the title because it is based on a 200-year-old recipe. Those five years are spent in French Limousin oak casks that had previously contained wine, and port pipes. There are stewed fruits on the nose and vanilla, oak and pepper on the palate. The distillers suggest that it can be enjoyed sipped neat, though it also makes a strong cocktail base.

Old Monk XXX Supreme

PRODUCER: Mohan Meakin

AREA OF ORIGIN: Mohan Nagar, India

VARIETY: Aged rum

ABV: 42.8%

WEBSITE: www.mohanmeakin.com

Old Monk rum is the collective name for a group of rums owned by Mohan Meakin, an Indian business that originally grew out of two separate beer brewery operations. These days, though, the company makes and owns a wide range of products, including spirits, juices and breakfast cereals. It owns three distilleries in all. XXX Supreme is a blend of old rum presented in a quirky monk-shaped bottle, so it makes a good present. The rum's quirky too. It is effectively an up-market version of the brewery's seven-year-old rum, and is dark, sweet and full-bodied, with notes of caramel, sweet spices and butterscotch.

Old Port East Indian

PRODUCER: Amrut

AREA OF ORIGIN: Bangalore, India

VARIETY: Dark rum

ABV: 42.8%

WEBSITE: www.amrutdistilleries.com

Amrut is something of a rarity because it makes single malt whisky using malted barley, unlike many of its competitors, which make something they call 'whisky', but which is made with molasses. And molasses is, of course, what rum is made with. You'd expect Amrut to know where the line is between the two spirits, and it does. Old Port East Indian is a very palatable example of a rum that the company exports, and which sells better abroad than it does in the domestic market. This is sweet with some spicy and woody notes. Better mixed than sipped straight.

Ord River Overproof Rum

PRODUCER: Hoochery Distillery

AREA OF ORIGIN: Kununurra, Australia

VARIETY: Gold rum

ABV: 56.4%

WEBSITE: www.hoochery.com.au

Hoochery Distillery is the oldest distillery in Western Australia and was the first to produce rum. It is owned by Raymond 'Spike' Dessert III, an American farmer who set up a seed business in the Ord River valley in The Kimberley, Western Australia, and took to the region with gusto. The region is ideal for producing sugarcane, and when the industry was booming and there was a surplus Spike hit upon the idea of making rum – Ord River Overproof Rum. This rum is full-bodied and its combination of spiciness, vanilla and chocolate notes make for a great sipping rum. It can be used to make an alternate version of an old-fashioned, too.

Phoenix Tears

PRODUCER: Firebox

AREA OF ORIGIN: West Indies

VARIETY: Spiced rum

ABV: 40.0%

WEBSITE: www.firebox.com

Firebox is an all-things-to-all-people sort of company, and specialises in gifting. Its journey into alcoholic spirits is a somewhat unconventional one, and this rum comes complete with hyperbolic marketing twaddle, a trendy looking bottle and lots of guff about secret recipes and bottling the tears of a mythical beast. Heritage and provenance are woefully in short supply, though the company does let pass that the rum is from the Caribbean and is 'premium'. According to the producers, the rum has 'aromas of brown sugar and dried fruit blended with natural cinnamon and ginger to give it a sweet and spicy flavour. It's the missing mythical ingredient in your liquor cabinet. Just give the bottle a shake and lose yourself as the shimmering golden embers swirl through an opalescent cosmos of dark and mysterious rum.'

Right.

Phraya Deep Matured

PRODUCER: International Beverage

AREA OF ORIGIN: Thailand

VARIETY: Gold rum

ABV: 40.0%

WEBSITE: www.phrayarum.com

International Beverage owns Inverhouse Distillers, which owns a handful of Scottish distilleries. The company has offices across South East Asia and is based in Hong Kong. But this rum is fromThailand. Phraya means 'high ranking' in Thai, and this rum is described as a 'super-premium Thai rum, distilled, matured, blended, and bottled in the Kingdom of Thailand. Deep matured over cool lagoons in oak barrels, this rum of distinction is beautifully balanced and seamlessly smooth.'

The rum is aged for between seven and 12 years and is matured over cold lakes to slow the maturation process down. The rum is packaged in a stylish and unmissable bottle. The rum is described as rich and complex, with vanilla, coconut, cloves, raisins, and with hints of caramel, pineapple and citrus.

Pirates Grog No. 13

PRODUCER: Pirates Grog

AREA OF ORIGIN: Roatán

VARIETY: Golden rum

ABV: 37.5%

WEBSITE: www.piratesgrogrum.com

Don't be put off by the trashy name, or the countless web reviews that can't resist the temptation to indulge in cliched pirate speak. This is actually a very serious rum with provenance and heritage in spades. It's described as a Honduran rum but it is actually put together on the island of Roatán, 60 kilometres away, haven for buccaneers in hiding or seeing off bad weather.

This is a single cask golden rum that has won a number of awards and, taste wise, is a total delight, with toffee and dark chocolate. It was created by Dutchman Robert J. van der Weg and is marketed by an English couple who discovered it while living in island splendour. A younger three-to-five-year-old rum from this company is also worth seeking out.

Plantation OFTD

PRODUCER: Maison Ferrand

AREA OF ORIGIN: Cognac, France

VARIETY: Dark rum

ABV: 69.0%

WEBSITE: www.plantationrum.com

OFTD stands for Old Fashioned Traditional Dark, and this meaty, beaty, big and bouncy rum is a blend of spirits from Guyana, Jamaica and Barbados. The French owners, in an exhibition of class, brought together a panel of experts that included American drinks expert David Wondrich and the owners of some of the world's best bars, including Trailer Happiness in London, and Latitude 29 in New Orleans to select the final rum. This rum joined the company portfolio in late 2016. This bursts with flavour, including raisins, nutmeg, oak, vanilla, molasses and honey. It has a particularly long finish, too.

Plantation XO 20th Anniversary

PRODUCER: Maison Ferrand

AREA OF ORIGIN: Barbados

VARIETY: Gold rum

ABV: 40.0%

WEBSITE: www.plantationrum.com

Plantation XO 20th Anniversary is owned by French Company Maison Ferrand and for this special rum to mark the 20th anniversary of the company, Barbadian spirit and French savoir faire were united. This is extraordinary; a selection of aged rum, some of it as old as 20 years, was matured in Barbados in ex-bourbon barrels, before being shipped to France. Once in France, it was further matured in small ex-Cognac barrels for another 12 to 18 months. The result is superb; toasted coconut and vanilla on the nose, and an orange crunchy bar on the palate – milk chocolate, honey and orange zest. The finish is rich and full.

Port Morant Demerara 1975

PRODUCER: Bristol Classic Rum Ltd

AREA OF ORIGIN: Guyana

VARIETY: Demerara rum

ABV: 46.0%

WEBSITE: www.classicrum.com

Port Morant is the oldest distiller at the Diamond Distillery and dates from an independent distillery called Port Morant, which was established in 1732. This vintage bottling is from Mayfair-based wine merchants Berry Bros. & Rudd, a company that has built up a highly respected collection of spirits. The company was founded in 1698, so it has a history stretching back even further than the distillery that produced this rum.

Rum distilled in the Caribbean evaporates at three times the rate of whisky made in the central belt of Speyside in the Scottish Highlands, so it's rare to get even a 20-year-old rum. This rum is over 30 years old. Port Morant products obtained by distillation are known to be a very strong, aromatic and oily distillate.

Pusser's 15 Year Old

PRODUCER: Pusser's Rum Ltd

AREA OF ORIGIN: Guyana and Trinidad

VARIETY: Dark rum

ABV: 40.0%

WEBSITE: www.pussersrum.com

The history of Pusser's is tied closely to that of the British Royal Navy. One of the longest traditions of the services was the granting of the daily tot of rum, which was given to the crew by the purser. The story goes that the name was adapted to pusser by the sailors. This is a blend of rums from Guyana and Trinidad made in century-old wooden stills. The rum is fermented naturally in open vats, where natural yeasts ferment the sugars. Fermentation is a three-stage process and takes 72 hours. The rum is then aged for 15 years in oak wood barrels. The full, rich flavour is all natural, and no flavouring agents are added. This is a big syrupy rum with lots of spice and vanilla.

Pusser's Gunpowder Proof

PRODUCER: Pusser's Rum Ltd

AREA OF ORIGIN: Guyana and Trinidad

VARIETY: Gold rum

ABV: 54.5%

WEBSITE: www.pussersrum.com

The tradition of giving the crews of England's battle ships a tot of rum every day started, incredibly, in 1655 and continued until 1970 – so it endured for more than 300 years. The strength of this daily rum was 54.5% ABV. Rum was given out partly because it was safer than drinking water and also because it killed a lot of germs. But life on warships in the 17th and 18th centuries was not for the faint-hearted. Battles were fought eyeball to eyeball, and the risk of injuries from splintered wood was very real. Rum helped settle the nerves. This rum was described by the editors of *Forbes* magazine as one of the top 10 rums in the world. It is rich in stewed and dried berry fruits, syrupy and with malt-like tannins. Beautiful.

Pyrat XO Reserve

PRODUCER: Patron Spirits Co.

AREA OF ORIGIN: Island of Aguia

VARIETY: Golden rum

ABV: 40.0%

WEBSITE: www.pyratrum.com

Never mind the spelling, this is another rum cosy-ing up to the Captain Sparrow image of rum. It's a blend of nine different pot still rums from the West Indies put together on the island of Aguia. The average age of the rums is 15 years old, but varies from eight to 40 years old, all aged in French oak casks. Aguilan rum has a history stretching back over 200 years. This rum is described by The Whisky Exchange website as a 'very special amber Caribbean blended rum. A real connoisseur's rum, with a sublimely orangey, spicy flavour and nuanced finish.'

Pyrat XO Reserve is hard to find because the distillery was closed. But this is a fine rum and is presented in a stylish wooden-barrel gift box.

Rebellion Spiced

PRODUCER: Dutch Spirits

AREA OF ORIGIN: Trinidad

VARIETY: Spiced rum

ABV: 37.5%

WEBSITE: www.rebellion-rum.com

Original producer Metaxa responded to a demand for a fuller tasting and spicier rum from its customers and created this. It's a fun brand but it's no novelty act. Ignore the website references to rebels and pirates and focus on the awards and high praise Rebellion Spiced has received. The rum is now part of a company based in Amsterdam, and is created by taking rum from a distillery in Trinidad and mixing it with fresh ingredients, including cloves, ginger, cardamom, pepper, vanilla, cinnamon and orange. This is another rum that can be enjoyed neat but is at its best when served with cola, ice, and a squeeze of fresh lime. One of the better spiced rums on the market.

Rhum Agricole Vieux Neisson

PRODUCER: Neisson Distillery

AREA OF ORIGIN: Martinique

VARIETY: Rhum agricole

ABV: 45.4%

WEBSITE: www.neisson.fr

Rhum is very different from commercial rums and can be something of an acquired taste. But the French have preferred it for more than 100 years and you'll find it in any self-respecting French bar, where it is often consumed on its own. It has a grassier, earthier, and oilier taste, and is considerably less artificial tasting and more complex than its molasses-fuelled cousins. It is often presented as an alternative to mescal. Rhum Agricole Vieux Niesson is widely regarded as one of the best examples of the drink. It is a blend of the distillery's best rums aged up to eight years. The age gives out body and weight and there are some very enjoyable fruity things going on in here, too.

MARTINIQUE

· DEPUIS 1932 ·
NEISSON
THIEUBERT CANARI

Le rhum VIEUX par Neisson

RHUM AGRICOLE MARTINIQUE
APPELLATION D'ORIGINE CONTRÔLÉE
RHUM VIEUX

MIS EN BOUTEILLE
AUX DOMAINES THIEUBERT
MARTINIQUE

45%VOL.

AGRICOLE

Rhum Barbancourt 15 Years Old Estate Reserve

PRODUCER: Societie du Rhum Barbancourt

AREA OF ORIGIN: Port au Prince, Haiti

VARIETY: Rhum agricole

ABV: 43.0%

WEBSITE: www.barbancourt.net

The French-speaking parts of the Caribbean make their rum in a different way to everyone else, making their spirit from sugarcane juice, as opposed to molasses. This defines a rhum agricole from a standard rum, but Rhum Barbancourt is different in another respect too; it undergoes a second distillation, giving it a substantially higher alcohol strength than most rums. It is reduced down to about 50.0% ABV and then put into a mixture of large oak vats and much smaller barrels. The resulting rum is a mixture of dried fruits, butterscotch and some oakiness. Although rhum agricole is a strong base for cocktails, at this age it's better to sip it straight over ice.

Ron Abuelo Centuria

PRODUCER: Varela Hermanos

AREA OF ORIGIN: Pesé, Panama

VARIETY: Gold rum

ABV: 40.0%

WEBSITE: www.ronabuelopanama.com

The history of Varela Hermanos dates back to 1908, when Don José Varela Blanco, a young Spanish immigrant, established the San Isidro Sugar Mill in the town of Pesé. The main activity of the town's population of about 10 000 people is the cultivation of sugarcane, and Varela Hermanos is the leading producer of distilled spirits in Panama.

Ron Abuelo Centuria is part of the company's Abuelo range, and was launched to mark the 100th anniversary of the founding of the sugar mill and the company. This is a special blend made up of Panamanian rums, some of which are up to 30 years old. The rum is matured in ex-Jack-Daniel's American white oak barrels and is produced using a solera system. It is complex, rich and bursting with flavour.

Ron Cartavio XO 18 Years Old

PRODUCER: Ron Cartavio Distillery

AREA OF ORIGIN: Cravat, Peru

VARIETY: Dark rum

ABV: 40.0%

WEBSITE: www.cartaviorumco.pe

Peru isn't the first place you think of when looking at rum production, but Ron Cartavio is both distinctive and very good. The distillery lies in the northern part of Peru and it credits the climate and humidity of the fertile valley of Chicamo, where the rums used in the XO 18-year-old XO are laid, to mature for its special character.

The distillery has been making rum since the early part of the 20th century and it is matured in American, French Limousin and Slovenian casks in a solera system. The rum that is produced this way is sweet, with buttery and spicy flavours. This is the oldest rum the distillery produces.

Ron Zacapa Centenario

PRODUCER: Rum Creation and Products

AREA OF ORIGIN: Guatemala

VARIETY: Aged rum

ABV: 40.0%

WEBSITE: www.zacaparum.com

Ron Zacapa is made by Rum Creation and Products, a subsidiary of Guatemala's biggest distillery, Industrias Licoreras de Guatemala, which produces a wide range of spirits. It was created at the beginning of the 20th century by two founding distillers who emigrated from Spain.

Ron Zacapa Centenario was first introduced in 1976 to mark the 100th anniversary of the founding of the Eastern Guatemalan town of Zacapa, and it is widely regarded as one of the best rums on the market. The rum is made by blending a range of rums created using a solera system, which means that as rum is taken from the bottom of the cask more rum is added at the top, ensuring an evolving spirit. It is matured in a mix of ex-sherry and ex-bourbon casks for a period of between six and 23 years. The results are highly impressive. It has won a slew of awards.

Royal Oak Trinidad Rum

PRODUCER: Angostura Holdings Limited

AREA OF ORIGIN: Trinidad and Tobago

VARIETY: Dark rum

ABV: 43.0%

WEBSITE: www.angostura.com

Angostura is of course most famous for its bitters, but actually it is a huge rum producer and this is just one of a large stable of different rums. Just as well really, as it has become a trend for the best drinks makers to make their own bitters or to seek out less familiar ones. Royal Oak Trinidad Rum is hand-crafted and matured for between five and seven years. Its owners say that Royal Oak has long been the staple rum for Trinidad and Tobago, and it is noted for its rounded and mellow taste. It's not the most sophisticated of rums, but the spicy notes are well suited to cocktail making, and it's very more-ish when drunk on its own.

Rum Sixty Six

PRODUCER: Foursquare Distillery

AREA OF ORIGIN: St Philip, Barbados

VARIETY: Aged rum

ABV: 43.0%

WEBSITE: www.rumsixtysix.com

Richard Searle's Foursquare Distillery manages to pull off a remarkable trick of producing world class rums in a traditional setting, but making them stylish and fashionable, and in step with today's fast-moving bar scene. If rum is to become a fashion item going forward, Richard Searle's rums will certainly be in the mix. The distillery, one of the last independently owned family distilleries, is sited on a pretty, and pretty impressive, estate, and it is big. It has a mix of pot and column stills, and makes a diverse range of rums. It is also very clean and environmentally friendly. In fact, what's not to love? Rum Sixty Six is distilled, aged and bottled here. It is distilled in small batches, usually 112 barrels, and is tropically aged for a minimum of 12 years in small American white oak casks. The result is a soft, rounded, slightly oaky sipping rum.

TROPICALLY AGED

TWELVE **12** YEARS

IMPORTED

TRADE **RUM** MARK

SIXTY SIX

Family Reserve

Distilled, Aged & Bottled at

FOURSQUARE DISTILLERY

ST. PHILIP BARBADOS

BARBADOS RUM

70cl 43% vol

Saint James 15 Year Old

PRODUCER: St James Distillery

AREA OF ORIGIN: Saint Pierre, Martinique

VARIETY: Rhum agricole

ABV: 42.0%

WEBSITE: www.saintjames-rum.com

This rum has its roots in a rum business set up by Father Edmund Lefebure in 1765. He was the superior of a convent on the island, but he was also a skilled businessman, and he began selling his rum to the British colonies in North America. This rum was originally called Jacques but the name was changed to make it more commercially British sounding. The rum is aged for a minimum of 15 years in small oak casks in the tropical ageing conditions of Martinique, for a high-end tasting experience. The result is an oaky and tannin-fuelled slow sipping rum, perfect to reflect back on a busy day.

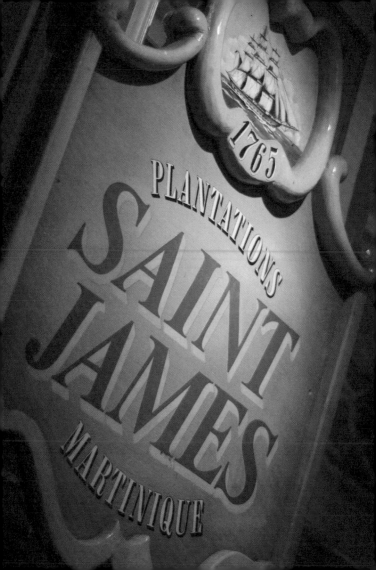

Saint James Cuvée 1765

PRODUCER: Saint James Plantations

AREA OF ORIGIN: Martinique

VARIETY: Dark rum

ABV: 43.0%

WEBSITE: www.saintjames-rum.com

Another rhum agricole from Martinique. Saint James Cuvée 1765 was produced on the 250th anniversary of the distillery. It was founded by a priest, Father Edmund Lefebure, who happened to be a skilled spirits maker. In order to sell his rum spirit to the residents of New England, he gave it an Anglo-Saxon name. This version is made of rums aged up to six years in small oak barrels. Great emphasis has been placed on producing a mellow and easy drinking rum, and the producers say it is dominated by spices and macerated fruits. This has been described as a good introduction to rhum agricole. And still we wait for the specialised rum market to become fashionable.

St. Nicholas Abbey 12 Year Old

PRODUCER: St. Nicholas Abbey

AREA OF ORIGIN: Barbados

VARIETY: Golden rum

ABV: 40.0%

WEBSITE: www.stnicholasabbey.com

St. Nicholas Abbey has a past stretching back to the very earliest days of sugar production and rum making on Barbados, one of several islands laying claim to be the one that invented the spirit. The distillery and plantation has been passed down through various families and has struggled through controversial times (slavery) and challenging ones (economic downturns). The Warren family took it over in 2006 and since then the family has restored the estate, including the distillery, and today it is one of just four on the island. The distillery makes rum using impressive-looking traditional equipment. Master distiller Richard Searle has introduced traditional recipes, too, and this 12-year-old is a beauty, all mellow toffee and chewy fruits.

Santa Teresa 1796

PRODUCER: Saint Teresa

AREA OF ORIGIN: Venezuela

VARIETY: Aged rum

ABV: 40.0%

WEBSITE: www.ronsantateresa.com

We play rugby, says the website. What? First things first. Santa Teresa makes some of the finest rum on the planet. But the distillery also recruits former gang members under its Alcatraz Project, which started when gang members tried to burgle the distillery by holding a security man at gunpoint. They were offered a choice of prison or work at the distillery. So successful and popular was the opportunity to reform that others have followed. And part of the rehabilitation programme is playing rugby as a bonding exercise. In fact, Venezuela's getting so good at rugby that the country was invited to send a sevens exhibition team to the World Sevens. 1796 is an all but faultless sipping rum from a distillery with impeccable social credentials. What's not to love?

Santa Teresa

1 7 9 6 ®

Ron Antiguo de Solera

Santiago de Cuba Añejo Rum

PRODUCER: Cuba Ron

AREA OF ORIGIN: Santiago, Cuba

VARIETY: Gold rum

ABV: 38.0%

WEBSITE: www.cubaron.com

For a while there we got a glimpse of what the world might look like if America lifted its travel and trade embargo on Cuba. Sadly, though, it would appear it was only a glimpse, and now the United States is disappearing back into its shell. But what would have happened to the world of rum if Cuba could compete freely? Where would that leave 'exiles' such as Bacardi, and how would Cuban producers fare in the global market?

We may never know now, but Santiago de Cuba Añejo Rum shows that the island may well be capable of providing a flood of quality Cuban whisky. Santiago de Cuba Añejo is from one of several state-owned distilleries, and is a peach. Añejo means 'aged' and this rum has been matured in white oak barrels for five years, resulting in a rum that is rich in vanilla, caramel and coffee flavours.

Seawolf White Rum

PRODUCER: Boilermaker Drinks Company

AREA OF ORIGIN: Edinburgh

VARIETY: White rum

ABV: 41.0%

WEBSITE: www.seawolfrum.com

Once it was all so straightforward: a distillery made a spirit, a drinks company marketed it and sold it, and bars made drinks with it. But modern trends have put paid to all that. These days the demand for a unique drink, a thirst for exciting and unusual flavours, and an interest in products with provenance and heritage, mean that a small bar is going to new extremes to provide a premium bespoke drinking experience. That's what Edinburgh's very cool bar Bramble has done. Bosses Mike Aikman and Jason Scott have teamed up with Gavin Ferguson, co-founder of Scottish independent wine merchants Vino Wines, to create this, a premium white rum distilled in Scotland. It's a cool looking, cool tasting and oily rum, ideal for the bar's cocktails but it's on sale too. How special is that?

Sparrow's Premium Aged Rum

PRODUCER: St Vincent Distillers Ltd

AREA OF ORIGIN: Georgetown, St Vincent

VARIETY: Dark rum

ABV: 40.0%

WEBSITE: www.sunsetrum.co.uk/the-rum/
sparrows-premium-aged-rum

Sunset Rum is something of an enigma in the world
of rum. On the one hand it is happy to indulge in the
fun side of the rum category, using pirate imagery
and brightly coloured labels to draw in younger club
and bar drinkers, but providing some very serious
quality rum. So on the one hand the company gives
us Captain Bligh, and on the other there's the very
serious Sunset Strong, which has an alcohol strength
of 84.5% ABV and is for responsible adults only.
Sparrow's sits somewhere between the two extremes.
The name recalls our pirate of the Caribbean friend
Jack, but this is an aged and extremely good rum.
It's distilled on a column still, matured in quality oak,
and is great value for money.

Spirits of Old Man Rum Project One

PRODUCER: Spirits of Old Man

AREA OF ORIGIN: Germany

VARIETY: Dark rum

ABV: 40.0%

WEBSITE: www.oldmanspirits.de

Spirits of Old Man is an independent bottler and, as the name suggests, this is the first of a series of special bottlings from it. There have been subsequent project releases that explore different rum styles. It is very difficult to find out much about the company, but this bottling, and subsequent project rums, have made it into international markets and have been sold through leading retailers. This is a beautifully packaged rum and is made by combining three rums, with one very young and one considerably older. The resulting rum is excellent, with an emphasis on dark chocolate and coffee notes. There are also some unusual smoky notes. Intriguing.

Spytail Black Ginger Rum

PRODUCER: Spytail

AREA OF ORIGIN: France

VARIETY: Spiced rum

ABV: 40.0%

WEBSITE: www.spytailrum.com

Spytail's website is enigmatic and vague, but claims that this spiced rum IS the spirit of adventure. There's a confusing maritime and travel theme to the site, and it's hard to follow its logic. No matter: this is an absolutely fabulous spiced rum. It's made to a centuries-old method of macerating fresh ginger root and an array of spices with the rum in the cask. The ginger and other spices dominate the taste, but there are some delicious tropical fruit notes, some honey and some toffee. Works well in cocktails or with fruit juices, but can equally be consumed on its own.

St Lucia 1931 Fourth Edition

PRODUCER: St Lucia Group of companies

AREA OF ORIGIN: Roseau, St Lucia

VARIETY: Dark rum

ABV: 43.0%

WEBSITE: www.saintluciarums.com

The St Lucia Group of Companies came into being in 1972. St Lucia had had a number of rum distilleries but most of them closed until only two remained, and they merged. Today there is just one small distillery site, but it is proud of the rums it makes and the emphasis it places on innovation and quality.

This fourth edition of the 1931 rum was released to mark the 83rd anniversary of rum production on St Lucia. It is a blend of rums aged between six and 12 years old and includes rums distilled in pot stills and coffey stills. This is an exquisite rum, with tropical fruit, some orange, and lots of spice.

Stone Pine Dead Man's Drop

PRODUCER: Stone Pine

AREA OF ORIGIN: Bathurst, Australia

VARIETY: Aged rum

ABV: 40.0%

WEBSITE: www.stonepinedistillery.com.au

Stone Pine distillery is run by Bev and Ian Glen, who have their roots in the Scottish brewing and distilling industry. Bev ran various Edinburgh pubs, and Ian holds a Post-Graduate Diploma in Brewing & Distilling from Heriot-Watt University, Edinburgh, and has spent his entire career in the malting, brewing and distilling industry.

The rum is intended to mark and symbolise an incident from Bathurst history. In 1830 members of the infamous Ribbon Gang were publicly hanged for murder, bush ranging and horse thieving. This was the first ever public hanging in Bathurst. Dead Man's Drop is a mixture of barrel-aged rum with orange peel, vanilla and the Australian native flavours of ringwood and cinnamon myrtle.

STONE PINE

ENTWISTLE · DUNN · DALEY
GAHAN · GLEESON · KEARNEY · KENNY
SHEPHERD · WEBSTER · DRIVER

DEAD MAN'S DROP

BLACK SPICED RUM

Stroh 80

PRODUCER: Stroh

AREA OF ORIGIN: Austria

VARIETY: Dark rum

ABV: 80.0%

WEBSITE: www.stroh.at

Yet another super-charged rum with a frightening alcohol strength. It's obviously not meant to be consumed on its own, and although there are stories of the spirit being used in biker initiation ceremonies, the Austrian producers are much happier to discuss the positive uses for this highly distinctive alcohol. From its colour to its taste, there is nothing even remotely like this rum. Its Austrian producers not only suggest you use it in cocktails and hot drinks but also as an accompaniment to Austrian delicacies such as Gugelhopf and Kaiserschmarron, or in baking and for flambés. If you decide to drink it straight, expect a hot spicy kick. Tastes great in cola.

Sunset Very Strong

PRODUCER: St Vincent Distillers Ltd

AREA OF ORIGIN: St Vincent and The Grenadines

VARIETY: White rum

ABV: 84.5%

WEBSITE: www.sunsetrum.com

Yes, you read that right – the strength of this rum is an eye-watering 84.5%, and this rum is designed to make a powerful base for cocktails. The island of St Vincent was once rich in sugarcane, and this distillery was originally set up to take advantage of that. Today the sugar refinery has gone and sugar is no longer the island's main export. This extraordinarily strong rum is the favoured spirit on the island of St Vincent, though for obvious reasons it is mixed by the locals with other ingredients. When a liberal dose of water is added this rum has buttered toast and tropical fruit notes as well as some ginger spice.

Sweetdram Smoked Spiced Rum

PRODUCER: Sweetdram

AREA OF ORIGIN: London

VARIETY: Spiced rum

ABV: 45.0%

WEBSITE: www.sweetdram.com

Sweetdram is a stylish spirits designer operating from East London, and will soon have a presence in Edinburgh too. It applies science and the Sweetdram team's technical skills to create new and exciting spirits drinks. Each creation may take months of research. The spirits themselves are then created by Sweetdram and a select number of carefully selected partners. So Smoked Spiced Rum is made alongside the very exciting and talented team at the East London Liquor Company. You can tell from the first sip that this is as much a work of art as a drink. Its base is a Demerara rum that has been infused with botanicals, including lapsang souchong, lime leaf, chamomile, cardamom, fennel, grains of paradise and fig. The result is a subtle, smoky, and very different rum.

Takamaka St André 8 Year Old

PRODUCER: Takamaka Bay Distillery

AREA OF ORIGIN: La Plaine St André, Seychelles

VARIETY:

ABV: 40.0%

WEBSITE: www.takamakarum.com

Takamaka Distillery is the brainchild of brothers Richard and Bernard d'Offay who opened the distillery in 2002 on the other side of the world to where the bulk of rum comes from, with the intention of making a genuinely different rum. They make a number of rums but the St André 8 Year Old is based on the brothers' grandfather's recipe. So is it any good? It sure is, and it has a clutch of awards and medals to prove it. It has been described as the most coveted rum in the Takamaka range, and among its fans are the chaps at online retailer Master of Malt, who were impressed by its creamy mouthfeel, its ginger spiciness and its toasted oak notes. And yes, it is a bit different.

The Real McCoy 5 Year Old

PRODUCER: Foursquare Distillery

AREA OF ORIGIN: St Philip, Barbados

VARIETY: Gold rum

ABV: 40.0%

WEBSITE: www.realmccoyspirits.com

The Real McCoy is named after Bill McCoy, who built his reputation for quality spirits during the Prohibition era, early in the last century. This rum, which is absolutely outstanding, has no added sugars, perfumes or flavourings, and it's made with pure spring water and the finest sugarcane. There are three in the range, aged for three, five or 12 years in heavily charred ex-bourbon barrels, and they taste as good as a fine bourbon or single malt whisky. The five year old makes fabulous value for money, and I strongly recommend you mix it with nothing. This is rich in vanilla, caramel and spice, with dried raisins, some treacle and lashings of oaky tannins. It is not sweet and cloying and if whisky is your thing, this rum is well worth exploring. The Real McCoy alright.

LEGENDARY RUM RUNNER

Bill McCoy

THE REAL McCOY®

SINGLE BLENDED RUM

with NO ADDED SUGAR, FLAVOR OR SPICE

A TRADITIONAL BARBADOS RUM
SMALL BATCH CRAFTED WITH
A UNIQUE BALANCE OF COPPER
COLUMN & POT STILLS

BLENDED WITH SPRING WATER &
GENUINELY SINGLE-CASK AGED
IN HEAVY CHAR AMERICAN OAK
BOURBON BARRELS

AGED

5

YEARS

FOURSQUARE DISTILLERY
ST. PHILIP, BARBADOS

PROOF
40% ALcVol (80 Proof)

QUANTITY
750mL / 75cL

BATCH NO
0516

The Real McCoy 12 Year Old

PRODUCER: Foursquare Distillery

AREA OF ORIGIN: St Philip, Barbados

VARIETY: Gold rum

ABV: 40.0%

WEBSITE: www.realmccoyspirits.com

The Real McCoy is named after Bill McCoy, who built his reputation for supplying quality spirits to the United States during Prohibition. He would sell unadulterated spirits offshore to customers who included speakeasy owners. Unlike many other unscrupulous suppliers, McCoy never interfered with his spirits and they became known for their superior quality. Visitors to speakeasies would seek them out, asking for the Real McCoy. This rum has no added sugars, perfumes or flavourings, and it's made with pure spring water and the finest sugarcane. This rum is matured for 12 years in heavily charred ex-bourbon barrels, and it's outstanding: rich in vanilla, caramel and spice, with dried raisins, some treacle and oaky tannins.

Trois Rivières Rhum Blanc

PRODUCER: Trois Rivières Distillery

AREA OF ORIGIN: Martinique

VARIETY: White rhum agricole

ABV: 50.0%

WEBSITE: www.plantationtroisrivieres.com

Ah, they were the days. Trois Rivières has roots stretching back to 1660, when Nicolas Fouquet, superintendent of finances under Louis XIV, awarded himself the largest plot of land ever allocated in the Antilles: 2,000 hectares in the south of the island. Some 125 years later rum production started there. Trois Rivières rum was established as an agricole rum in 1940, and although the distillery has moved, it has continued to make a distinctive iconic rhum ever since. This is a stronger version of rhum blanc, and is a great example of a premium white rum. It's sweet and strong but with a pungent thump of a finish. Agricole rhum at its best.

Valdespino Ron Viejo

PRODUCER: José Estévez

AREA OF ORIGIN: Jerez, Spain

VARIETY: Aged rum

ABV: 43.0%

WEBSITE: www.grupoestevez.es

It's not every rum website that has a link to a stud farm, but then there's nothing very normal about the Estévez Group. For a starter, the company is best known for its wines, and particularly its sherries. It markets a wide range of products, which includes malt whisky, and it caters for the wine tourist on its extensive bodega in Jerez. Valdespino Ron Viejo was brought to Jerez for aging after it was given to the Estévez Group as a present by one of the Cuban-run companies it provided sherry butts for. It was set up in a sherry butt solera system so the average age is about 20 years. This is excellent.

Watson's Trawler Rum

PRODUCER: Ian MacLeod Distillers

AREA OF ORIGIN: Babados and Guyana

VARIETY: Dark rum

ABV: 40.0%

WEBSITE: www.ianmacleod.com

Ian MacLeod Distillers is an independent family firm that owns a portfolio of top-quality brands as well as the single malt distilleries Tamdhu and Glengoyne. Rum doesn't spring to mind when you think about the company, but Watson's Trawler Rum has been quietly achieving success over the years, and is well placed to now take advantage of the renewed interest in the category. It is made up of Demerara rums from Guyana and rums from Barbados. The individual rums are matured in oak casks before they are blended together. Perhaps surprisingly, Watson's is part of a healthy market for dark navy-style rums in Scotland, with several Scottish independent bottlers producing dark rums. This dark rum has a history stretching back 100 years, and offers extremely good value for money.

Westerhall Estate Rum No. 10

PRODUCER: Westerhall Estate

AREA OF ORIGIN: Grenada

VARIETY: Gold rum

ABV: 40.0%

WEBSITE: www.westerhallrums.co.uk

Westerhall Estate is a distinguished and highly respected rum producer based in Guyana; its name is said to have come from the name of the Scottish ancestral home of Sir William Johnstone, who first owned the estate.

Westerhall Estate Rum No. 10 is the jewel in the company's crown. It was launched in 2016 to replace the company's Vintage Rum as part of a company brand overhaul. It is a silky smooth and rounded rum that can be sipped over ice, though the the traditional way of drinking it in Guyana is with coconut juice. It has an unusual taste, with honey, oak, baked apple and spice all vying for attention.

Wood's 100 Old Navy

PRODUCER: William Grant & Sons

AREA OF ORIGIN: Guyana

VARIETY: Dark rum

ABV: 57.0%

WEBSITE: www.williamgrant.com

The 100 in the name of this rum refers to 100 proof under the British proofing system – that's 57% ABV, and this is the strength a spirit needs to be before a match will ignite gunpowder soaked in the rum. There is a strong naval link with Wood's and the idea behind this expression was to create a naval rum in a traditional manner. Wood's 100 Old Navy and the spirit is made with the rich sugarcane taken from the banks of the Demerara River. It is distilled into three separate rums, which are then blended together. This has a rich syrupy taste and is remarkably smooth, with toffee and spice notes. It makes a strong cocktail base.

Wray & Nephew White Overproof

PRODUCER: Gruppo Campari

AREA OF ORIGIN: Jamaica

VARIETY: White rum

ABV: 63.0%

WEBSITE: www.jwrayandnephew.com

Gruppo Campari has been expanding considerably in recent years and has added Scottish single malt, Irish whiskey and American bourbon distilleries to its portfolio. But it seems to have a pretty honourable attitude towards its acquisitions, investing to improve them, and staying away from the day-to-day running of them. Wray & Nephew is no exception. White Overproof is the world's biggest selling over-strength rum, and is a special blend of rums from Wray & Nephew's estates. It has a fruity natural aroma with overtones of molasses, and the palate is complex, with exotic fruits and banana. It's fiery, with a long spicy finish.

Zacapa XO

PRODUCER: Rum Creation and Products

AREA OF ORIGIN: Guatemala

VARIETY: Dark rum

ABV: 40.0%

WEBSITE: www.zacaparum.com

Another extraordinary rum from a country that doesn't come over as a premium producer. Zacapa XO is a super premium blended rum containing rums aged for between six and 25 years. The rum is matured in ex-bourbon and sherry casks in the mountains above the distillery, where the temperature is more consistent and lower, making for a slower maturation. An extra maturation process in former French Cognac casks ensures a richer, fuller and spicier rum. The big range of ages in the rums used is due to the use of a process unique to Zacapa, called the Sistema Solera. The resulting rum is very up front and intense, with tobacco and carpenter shop notes, and syrupy fruit.

Zuidam Flying Dutchman Rum 1

PRODUCER: Zuidam

AREA OF ORIGIN: Baarle Nassau, Netherlands

VARIETY: White rum

ABV: 40.0%

WEBSITE: www.zuidam.eu

Zuidam is a family owned Dutch company that makes hundreds of different whiskies, fruit liqueurs, genevers and assorted spirits. The quality of the distillery is exceptional, with fresh fruit and the best herbs, spices and botanicals all used to ensure the finest quality. Rum isn't commonly made in Europe, but if anyone's going to do it, it's Zuidam. As with many of the distillery's spirits and liqueurs, Flying Dutchman Rum 1 is exceptionally well made, distinctive and different. It's made with pure cane molasses, is triple distilled and matured in oak for six months. This is a premium sipping rum, and is significantly different to the caramel sweet Caribbean rums. It has a more earthy flavour, with some citrus notes.

Index

Picture Credits

The publishers would like to thank the following for their assistance with images:

Ableforth's, Alnwick, Amrut, Boilermaker Drinks Company, Clement Rhum, Cloven Hoof Rum (Guilty Libations Ltd), Cuba Ron Corporation S.A., Dark Matter Distillers, Demerara Distillers Limited, Diageo, Diplomatico / Destilerías Unidas S. A., Emporia Brands, Hoochery Distillery, Island Company Rum, José Estévez S.A., Licores Veracruz, Matthew Clark, Neisson, Outerbanks Distilling, Pirate's Grog Rum, Real McCoy Spirits, Corp., Ron Abuelo, St Nicholas Abbey, St. Vincent Distilleries Ltd, Stoli Group, Stone Pine Distillery, Strathearn Distillery, Stroh, Sweetdram, Takamaka Rum, The Patrón Spirits Company, Westerhall Rum, Zuidam Distillers BV

Andrew Currie (CC BY 2.0), Dominic Lockyer (CC BY 2.0), Erik Cleves Kristensen (CC BY 2.0), Flor de Caña Rum (CC BY-SA 3.0), Lars Schmidt (CC BY-SA 3.0), Lyman Erskine (CC BY 2.0), Nigab Pressbilder (CC BY 2.0), Rfultz (CC BY 2.0)

Aneta Waberska, Anton_Ivanov, Brent Hofacker, Chef photography, gresei, gueriero093, Jorge Casais, Keith Homan, KIMKUNG, kizer13, lidian Neeleman, Lucia Pitter, manjagui, marcin jucha, Matyas Rehak, mbrand85, monticello, Myroslava, nelea33 Oliver Hoffmann, SeaRick1, The Visual Explorer, Tony Baggett / ALL Shutterstock

BANANA PANCAKE, BanPanPix, Chronicle, drink Alan King, FORRAY Didier/SAGAPHOTO.COM, Hemis / ALL Alamy Stock Photo

Collins

LITTLE BOOKS

These beautifully presented Little Books make excellent pocket-sized guides, packed with hints and tips.

Bananagrams Secrets
978-0-00-825046-1
£6.99

Bridge Secrets
978-0-00-825047-8
£6.99

101 ways to win at Scrabble
978-0-00-758914-2
£6.99

Craft Beer
978-0-00-827120-6
£6.99

Gin
978-0-00-825810-8
£6.99

Whisky
978-0-00-825108-6
£6.99

Scottish Castles
978-0-00-825111-6
£6.99

Scottish Dance
978-0-00-821056-4
£6.99

Scottish History
978-0-00-825110-9
£6.99

Clans and Tartans
978-0-00-825109-3
£6.99

Available to buy from all good booksellers and online.
All titles are also available as ebooks.
www.collins.co.uk

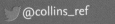 @collins_ref   facebook.com/collinsref